FE Other Discipline

Copyright © 2024 by Dusty R. Zimmerman, Blue Prep Academy

This text is designed to provide accurate and reliable information about the subject matter it covers. The publisher sells it without promising to provide specialized services like accounting or legal advice. If such professional guidance is needed, one should consult a qualified expert in that field.

This content is based on a set of principles endorsed by both a committee from the American Bar Association and one from a group of Publishers and Associations. Reproducing, copying, or sharing any part of this document through electronic or printed means is illegal. Recording or storing this publication without the publisher's written consent is strictly forbidden. All rights are reserved. The information given is believed to be honest and stable, with the understanding that any liability for negligence or otherwise, arising from the use or misuse of any information, policies, or instructions in this document, lies entirely with the reader. The publisher is not liable for any losses or damages, direct or indirect, that may result from the use of the information provided. Copyrights not held by the publisher belong to the respective authors. The information is meant for informational purposes only and is not presented with any guarantee or warranty. Trademarks mentioned are used without permission, and their publication does not imply endorsement by the trademark owner. All trademarks and brands mentioned in this book are used for identification purposes only and belong to their respective owners, not associated with this publication.

FE Other Disciplines Exam Prep

The All-in-One Study Guide with Practical Problems and Detailed Solutions to Get Ready in Less Than a Month and Pass with a 98% Success Rate on Your First Try

Dusty R. Zimmerman
- Blue Prep Academy -

Table of Contents

Introduction	8
Overview of the FE Other Disciplines Exam	8
Chapter 1: Mathematics	10
Analytic Geometry and Trigonometry	10
Differential Equations	11
Numerical Methods	13
Linear Algebra	14
Single-variable Calculus	16
Problems:	19
Solutions:	20
Chapter 2: Probability and Statistics	23
Estimation Techniques	23
Expected Value and Decision Making	24
Sampling Distributions	26
Goodness of Fit Tests	28
Problems:	30
Solutions:	30
Chapter 3: Chemistry	32
Oxidation and Reduction	32
Acids and Bases	33
Chemical Reactions	35
Problems:	38
Solutions:	39
Chapter 4: Instrumentation and Controls	41
Sensors	41
Data Acquisition Systems	43
Logic Diagrams:	44
Problems:	47
Solutions:	47
Chapter 5: Engineering Ethics and Societal Impacts	49
Codes of Ethics	49
Public Protection Issues	50
Societal Impacts of Engineering Decisions	52

Problems:	55
Solutions:	55

Chapter 6: Safety, Health, and Environment — 57

Industrial Hygiene	57
Safety Equipment	58
Gas Detection and Monitoring	60
Electrical Safety	62
Confined Space Entry	63
Hazard Communications	65
Problems:	67
Solutions:	67

Chapter 7: Engineering Economics — 69

Time Value of Money	69
Cost Analysis	70
Economic Analysis Techniques	72
Dealing with Uncertainty in Economic Analysis	73
Project Selection Methods	75
Problems:	77
Solutions:	77

Chapter 8: Statics — 79

Vector Analysis	79
Force Systems	80
Equilibrium of Rigid Bodies	82
Internal Forces	83
Area Properties	84
Static Friction	86
Free-Body Diagrams	87
Weight and Mass Computations	89
Problems:	92
Solutions:	92

Chapter 9: Dynamics — 94

Kinematics of Particles and Rigid Bodies	94
Linear and Angular Motion	95
Impulse and Momentum	97

Work, Energy, and Power	99
Dynamic Friction	101
Vibrations	102
Problems:	105
Solutions:	105
Chapter 10: Strength of Materials	**107**
Stress and Strain Types	107
Combined Loading	108
Beam, Truss, Frame, and Column Analysis	110
Shear and Moment Diagrams	112
Material Failure Theories	114
Problems:	116
Solutions:	116
Chapter 11: Materials	**118**
Properties of Materials	118
Material Selection:	120
Problems:	122
Solutions:	122
Chapter 12: Fluid Mechanics	**124**
Fluid Properties	124
Dynamics:	125
Flow in Pipes and Open Channels:	127
Fluid Measurement and Machinery	129
Problems:	131
Solutions:	132
Chapter 13: Basic Electrical Engineering	**134**
Electrical Fundamentals	134
Circuit Laws and Analysis	136
AC and DC Circuits	137
Electrical Measurement Devices	139
Three-Phase Systems	140
Problems:	143
Solutions:	143
Chapter 14: Thermodynamics and Heat Transfer	**145**

Thermodynamic Laws and Equilibrium	145
Thermodynamic Properties and Processes	146
Heat Transfer Methods	148
Psychrometrics	150
Problems:	153
Solutions:	153
Conclusion	157

Introduction

Overview of the FE Other Disciplines Exam

The Fundamentals of Engineering (FE) Other Disciplines Exam is a cornerstone for any engineer seeking to lay a robust foundation for their professional career. It represents a critical rite of passage that transitions theoretical knowledge into the practical world of licensed engineering. This exam is uniquely designed to test a broad spectrum of skills and knowledge across various engineering disciplines, making it ideal for those whose academic background or professional aspirations span multiple fields.

The Essence of the FE Exam

Administered by the National Council of Examiners for Engineering and Surveying (NCEES®), the FE Other Disciplines Exam is the gateway to obtaining the much-coveted Engineer in Training (EIT) or Engineering Intern (EI) certification. This certification is universally recognized across the United States and serves as the first step toward earning a Professional Engineer (PE) license.

What Makes the FE Other Disciplines Unique?

Unlike other FE exams that focus on specific disciplines like civil or mechanical engineering, the FE Other Disciplines Exam encompasses a broader range of topics. It covers essential subjects from mathematics and material science to ethics and business practices, reflecting the diverse skill set required in the multifaceted world of engineering. This wide-ranging approach ensures that candidates are well-rounded in their foundational engineering knowledge, prepared to tackle complex problems in any field.

Structure and Format of the FE Other Disciplines Exam

Understanding the structure and format of the FE Other Disciplines Exam is crucial for effective preparation and success on exam day. The exam's design is meticulously crafted to assess both breadth and depth of knowledge across various engineering fields, making it unique among the Fundamentals of Engineering exams.

Detailed Breakdown of the Exam Format

Exam Duration and Scheduling: The FE Other Disciplines Exam is a six-hour long computer-based test, which includes several components:

- **Tutorial (8 minutes):** Before the exam begins, you will be given a short tutorial that explains how to navigate through the exam. This includes understanding how to mark questions for review and how to ensure your answers are saved.

- **Actual Exam Time (5 hours and 20 minutes):** During this period, you will answer 110 multiple-choice questions. These questions are split into two sections, with a scheduled break in between.

- **Scheduled Break (25 minutes):** After the first 55 questions, you are permitted a 25-minute break. It's important to note that the break is optional, but taking it can help you recharge before tackling the second half of the exam.

Question Format and Session Details:

- **Multiple-Choice Questions:** Each question provides four possible answers from which you must select the correct one. The questions are designed to test your understanding and ability to apply concepts in real-world scenarios.

- **Adaptive Complexity:** The difficulty of the questions may adapt based on your performance as you proceed through the exam. Early questions determine the level of subsequent questions, making it vital to stay focused and accurate from the start.

The Significance of Passing the FE Exam

Passing the FE Other Disciplines Exam paves the way to professional practice and is often a prerequisite for advanced engineering positions and responsibilities. It signals to employers, peers, and the public that an individual is committed to maintaining and enhancing the quality of engineering work, adhering to a strict ethical code, and continually updating their technical knowledge. Achieving a passing score is not just a personal triumph but a professional endorsement of an engineer's skills and dedication to their craft.

In essence, the FE Other Disciplines Exam is more than just a test; it is a milestone that marks the beginning of a lifelong journey in engineering, characterized by growth, learning, and commitment to excellence. It sets the stage for aspiring engineers to embark on a rewarding path that shapes not only their careers but also the future of innovation and development in the engineering world.

Chapter 1: Mathematics

Analytic Geometry and Trigonometry

Analytic geometry and trigonometry are fundamental branches of mathematics that play a critical role in various engineering fields. Analytic geometry, also known as coordinate geometry, merges algebra and geometry to solve problems involving points, lines, and curves by using coordinates and equations. Trigonometry, on the other hand, deals with the relationships between the angles and sides of triangles, particularly right triangles, and extends these concepts to periodic functions used to model real-world phenomena.

Key Concepts in Analytic Geometry

1. The Cartesian Coordinate System: The Cartesian coordinate system is the backbone of analytic geometry, providing a framework to describe the position of points or the arrangement of shapes in a two-dimensional space using x and y coordinates. This system can be extended into three dimensions for more complex applications in engineering such as in the design and analysis of structures or the tracking of moving objects.

2. Equations of Lines and Slopes: Understanding how to derive and manipulate the equations of lines is crucial. The slope-intercept form $y = mx + b$, where mmm is the slope and b is the y-intercept, is one of the simplest and most used forms. Another important form is the point-slope form, which is used for constructing a line given a point and a slope.

3. Circles and Ellipses: The equations for circles and ellipses are fundamental in fields such as optics and satellite tracking. The standard form for a circle centered at (h,k) with radius r is $(x-h)^2 + (y-k)^2 = r^2$, and for an ellipse, it is $\frac{(x-h)^2}{a^2} + \frac{(y-k)^2}{b^2} = 1$, where a and b are the distances from the center to the vertices along the major and minor axes, respectively.

4. Hyperbolas and Parabolas: These conic sections are vital in understanding the paths of celestial bodies and designing structures like parabolic antennas or bridges. The standard equation for a parabola can vary depending on its orientation and whether it is shifted from the origin, but it generally takes the form $y = ax^2 + bx + c$ for a vertical parabola.

Fundamental Concepts in Trigonometry

1. Trigonometric Functions: The primary trigonometric functions—sine, cosine, and tangent—are essential for calculating unknown angles and distances in right triangles, which is particularly useful in fields such as surveying and architecture. The functions are also extended to the unit circle, which allows them to be applied to any angle, beyond the initial 0° to 90° range.

2. Trigonometric Identities: Several identities exist that can simplify calculations and solve equations, including the Pythagorean identity $(0 + 0 = 1)$ and angle sum identities, $\sin(\alpha + \beta) = \sin \alpha \cos \beta + \cos \alpha \sin \beta$. These identities are indispensable tools in engineering problems involving oscillations and waves.

3. Law of Sines and Cosines: These laws generalize the rules of right triangles to any triangle. The Law of Sines, $\frac{\sin \alpha}{a} = \frac{\sin \beta}{b} = \frac{\sin Y}{c}$, and the Law of Cosines, $c^2 = a^2 + b^2 - 2ab \cos \cos Y$, are especially useful in triangulation, a technique used in GPS technology and robotics.

4. Inverse Trigonometric Functions: These functions, including arcsine, arccosine, and arctangent, are used to determine an angle from a ratio of sides, facilitating the backward calculation necessary in many engineering designs and applications.

Applications in Engineering

The application of analytic geometry and trigonometry is vast in engineering. For example, in civil engineering, trigonometry helps in calculating the correct angles and dimensions needed to construct stable structures like bridges and buildings. In electrical engineering, trigonometry is used to study the behavior of alternating currents.

Analytic geometry is also used extensively in mechanical engineering for designing and analyzing complex systems that require precise calculations of moving parts within machinery or for space optimization in product design.

Conclusion

A solid understanding of analytic geometry and trigonometry is essential for any aspiring engineer preparing for the FE Other Disciplines Exam. These mathematical tools not only support various engineering tasks but also foster a deeper understanding of the physical world, enabling engineers to innovate and solve complex problems efficiently.

Differential Equations

Differential equations are a powerful tool in mathematics and engineering, providing essential methods for modeling and solving problems involving rates of change and dynamic systems. They form the backbone of many engineering disciplines, from mechanical and aerospace to electrical and chemical engineering, by describing how physical quantities evolve over time or space.

Understanding Differential Equations

1. Basics of Differential Equations: A differential equation is an equation that involves an unknown function and its derivatives. These equations can be classified based on their order, the highest derivative present, and linearity. The simplest form is a first-order linear differential equation, while more complex systems may involve higher-order and nonlinear differential equations.

2. Types of Differential Equations:

- **Ordinary Differential Equations (ODEs):** These involve functions of a single variable and their derivatives. They are extensively used to model the behavior of physical systems, from the motion of planets to the dynamics of electrical circuits.

- **Partial Differential Equations (PDEs):** These involve functions of multiple variables and their partial derivatives. Examples include the heat equation, which models temperature distribution over time, and the wave equation, which describes the propagation of waves.

Solving Differential Equations

1. Analytical Methods: Some differential equations can be solved explicitly through analytical methods, which provide exact solutions. Techniques include separation of variables, integrating factors, and characteristic equations for linear differential equations. For ODEs, solutions might involve finding an integrating factor or using special techniques for exact or Bernoulli equations.

2. Numerical Methods: When analytical solutions are not feasible, numerical methods come into play. These methods approximate solutions at discrete points and are crucial in handling real-world engineering problems where exact solutions are impractical. Common numerical methods include Euler's method, Runge-Kutta methods, and finite difference methods for PDEs.

3. Laplace Transforms: Laplace transforms are another powerful tool for solving linear differential equations, especially those with variable coefficients and non-homogeneous terms. This technique transforms a differential equation in the time domain into an algebraic equation in the Laplace domain, which is often simpler to solve.

Applications in Engineering

Differential equations are integral to engineering analysis and design, providing a mathematical framework for modeling and solving complex systems:

- **Mechanical Engineering:** In mechanical systems, differential equations model everything from the vibrations of structures to the dynamics of fluids. For example, the differential equations governing the motion of a pendulum can predict its behavior under various forces.

- **Electrical Engineering:** In electrical circuits, the relationship between voltage, current, and resistance can be expressed using differential equations, especially in circuits involving capacitors and inductors where charges and currents change over time.

- **Chemical Engineering:** Reaction kinetics, which are crucial for designing reactors and understanding reaction mechanisms, are often modeled using differential equations that describe the rate of reaction as a function of concentration and time.

- **Civil Engineering:** The analysis of load-bearing structures often involves solving differential equations to ensure stability under dynamic loads, such as those experienced during earthquakes.

- **Environmental Engineering:** The dispersion of pollutants in air or water, crucial for assessing environmental impacts, can be modeled using PDEs that account for variables like wind speed and water currents.

Advanced Topics in Differential Equations

As engineers progress in their careers, more complex differential equations may be encountered, such as nonlinear systems that describe chaotic systems in aerodynamics or advanced materials science. Mastery of differential equations also involves understanding stability and chaos theory, which can be critical when designing systems that must operate under a wide range of conditions.

Conclusion

Differential equations are not just mathematical expressions but are the language of engineers in describing and solving real-world problems. Understanding how to formulate, solve, and apply differential equations is essential for success in the FE Other Disciplines Exam and beyond. This chapter aims to equip you with the foundational knowledge and problem-solving skills necessary to handle differential equations confidently in both your exam and professional engineering practice.

Numerical Methods

Numerical methods are essential techniques in engineering that allow the approximation of complex mathematical problems which cannot be solved analytically. They are critical in simulating, predicting, and optimizing systems across all fields of engineering, from designing aircraft to predicting weather patterns.

Core Concepts in Numerical Methods

1. Importance of Numerical Methods: Numerical methods provide solutions to differential equations, integrations, matrix operations, and other mathematical problems through iterative approximations. This approach is vital when exact answers are impossible or impractical to determine due to the complexity or non-linearity of the equation involved.

2. Characteristics of Numerical Methods: These methods are designed to handle precision, error propagation, and computational efficiency. Understanding the balance between accuracy and computational cost is crucial in engineering applications where large-scale simulations are performed.

Fundamental Techniques in Numerical Methods

1. Root Finding: One of the first problems tackled by numerical methods is finding roots of equations. Techniques such as the Bisection method, Newton-Raphson method, and Secant method are popular. Each has its advantages and suitability depending on the function's behavior and the required precision.

- **Bisection Method:** This method is simple and robust, used when you know the function changes sign over an interval. It repeatedly bisects the interval and selects a subinterval in which the function changes sign until it closes in on the root.

- **Newton-Raphson Method:** This is a faster method that uses derivatives to rapidly converge to a root, ideal for well-behaved functions but requiring a good initial guess.

- **Secant Method:** Similar to Newton-Raphson but does not require the derivative of the function, making it useful when derivatives are difficult to calculate.

2. Numerical Integration and Differentiation: Many engineering problems involve calculating integrals and derivatives where analytical solutions are not feasible.

- **Trapezoidal Rule and Simpson's Rule:** These are methods for numerical integration that approximate the area under a curve by dividing it into trapezoids or parabolic segments, respectively.

- **Finite Difference Method:** Used for numerical differentiation, this method approximates derivatives by using differences between function values at specific points.

3. Linear Algebraic Equations: Solving systems of linear equations is fundamental in engineering for analyzing structures, fluid dynamics, and electrical circuits.

- **Gaussian Elimination:** A method for solving linear equations by transforming the system into an upper triangular matrix, then performing back substitution.

- **LU Decomposition:** This involves decomposing a matrix into the product of a lower triangular and an upper triangular matrix, which simplifies solving multiple systems with the same coefficient matrix.

- **Iterative Methods:** Techniques like the Jacobi method, Gauss-Seidel method, and Conjugate Gradient method are crucial for large systems where direct methods are computationally expensive.

4. Ordinary Differential Equations (ODEs) and Partial Differential Equations (PDEs): Numerical methods are often the only practical way to solve complex differential equations used to model real-world phenomena in engineering.

- **Euler's Method:** A straightforward approach for solving first-order ODEs, providing a step-by-step procedure to approximate the solution.

- **Runge-Kutta Methods:** These provide a more accurate solution than Euler's method by considering additional points at each step.

- **Finite Element Method (FEM):** Used for solving PDEs, particularly in complex shaped domains or where the exact solutions are not available.

Applications and Implications

Numerical methods are applied in virtually every aspect of engineering. For instance, in civil engineering, they are used to simulate the load distribution in structures. In aerospace engineering, numerical solutions to fluid dynamics equations help design more efficient aircraft. Environmental engineers use these methods to model pollution dispersion and groundwater flow.

Conclusion

Mastery of numerical methods is essential for any engineer preparing for the FE Other Disciplines Exam. This chapter has provided a foundational understanding of the key techniques and their applications, ensuring you are well-prepared to tackle numerical problems effectively. Understanding these methods will not only help you in examinations but also in practical engineering problems where analytical solutions are often unfeasible.

Linear Algebra

Linear algebra is a fundamental branch of mathematics that is essential in nearly all areas of engineering. It deals with vectors, matrices, and linear transformations, providing tools for modeling and solving complex systems that can be represented in linear form. This field is crucial for understanding systems dynamics, structural analysis, electrical circuits, and much more.

Key Concepts in Linear Algebra

1. Vectors and Vector Spaces: Vectors are not just quantities with magnitude and direction; they are elements of vector spaces—sets in which vectors are added together and multiplied ("scaled") by numbers, called scalars in this context. In engineering, vectors are used to represent physical quantities such as forces, velocities, and fields.

2. Matrices and Determinants: A matrix is a rectangular array of numbers, symbols, or expressions, arranged in rows and columns. The determinant of a matrix is a scalar value that can be computed from the elements of a square matrix and encodes certain properties of the matrix. Determinants are useful in analyzing matrix invertibility, solving linear equations, and changing variable in integrals.

3. Systems of Linear Equations: Linear algebra provides methods for solving systems of linear equations, which is a common requirement in all fields of engineering. These systems can be represented in matrix form as Ax=b, where A is a matrix of coefficients, x is a column vector of variables, and b is a column vector of constants.

Solving Linear Systems

1. Matrix Operations:

- **Addition and Multiplication:** Basic operations that follow specific rules. Matrix multiplication, in particular, is not commutative, meaning that AB≠BA in general.

- **Inverse:** The matrix inverse of A is denoted as A^{-1} and is particularly important because, when it exists, it can be used to find solutions to systems of equations Ax=b by multiplying both sides by A^{-1}

2. Rank and Nullity:

- **Rank:** The dimension of the vector space generated (or spanned) by the column vectors of the matrix. It gives us insights into the solution set of the linear system.

- **Nullity:** The dimension of the kernel of A, which is the set of all vectors xxx such that Ax=0. Rank and nullity together give a deep insight into the nature of the solutions that the system might have.

3. Eigenvalues and Eigenvectors: These are instrumental in understanding matrix transformations. An eigenvector of a matrix A is a non-zero vector that changes by only a scalar factor when that matrix is applied to it. The corresponding scalar is called an eigenvalue. This concept is critical in many applications, including stability analysis, quantum mechanics, and population models.

Applications in Engineering

Linear algebra's applications in engineering are vast and varied:

- **Structural Engineering:** Analysis of structures using techniques such as the stiffness matrix method, where forces and displacements are related linearly.

- **Electrical Engineering:** Circuits can be analyzed using Kirchhoff's laws, which can be formulated as systems of linear equations solvable via matrix operations.

- **Control Engineering:** Design and analysis of control systems often involve dealing with systems of differential equations that can be discretized and represented in matrix form.

- **Computer Graphics:** Transformations in 3D space, including rotations, scaling, and translations, are performed using matrices.

Advanced Topics in Linear Algebra

In higher-level engineering, linear algebra can be extended to deal with complex numbers and spaces of higher dimensions, which are not typically covered in introductory texts but are crucial in specific fields like quantum computing and advanced electromagnetics.

Conclusion

Linear algebra is not just a set of mathematical tools but is the language of modern engineering, providing a framework that underpins both theoretical and practical applications in technology and science. Understanding the depth and applications of linear algebra will equip you with the necessary skills to tackle both the FE exam and professional engineering challenges effectively. This chapter aims to build a solid foundation in linear algebra, emphasizing its practical applications in engineering to ensure you are well-prepared for both your exam and future career endeavors.

Single-variable Calculus

Single-variable calculus is a core component of mathematical education in engineering, providing the tools to describe and analyze dynamically changing systems. This area of mathematics focuses on functions of one variable and includes the study of limits, derivatives, integrals, and the Fundamental Theorem of Calculus. These concepts are crucial for modeling physical phenomena, optimizing engineering designs, and solving practical problems in real-time scenarios.

Key Concepts in Single-variable Calculus

1. Functions and Limits:

- **Functions:** A function f in calculus is typically a rule that assigns a unique output f(x) for every input xxx. Understanding how functions behave, and how they can be manipulated, is fundamental to calculus.
- **Limits:** The concept of a limit is essential in calculus. It describes the behavior of a function as it approaches a certain point. Limits help in understanding discontinuities and the behavior of functions at points not easily evaluated by direct substitution.

2. The Derivative:

- **Definition:** The derivative of a function at a point gives the rate at which the function's value changes with respect to changes in the input value. It is defined as the limit of the difference quotient as the interval approaches zero.
- **Interpretation:** In practical terms, derivatives represent rates of change, such as velocity, which is the derivative of position with respect to time.
- **Techniques of Differentiation:** These include the power rule, product rule, quotient rule, and chain rule. Each technique is essential for finding the derivatives of various kinds of functions encountered in engineering tasks.

3. Applications of Derivatives:

- **Optimization:** Derivatives are used to find local maxima and minima of functions, an essential task in engineering for optimizing performance, cost, and resources.
- **Curve Sketching:** Understanding the behavior of functions, including intervals of increase and decrease, concavity, and points of inflection, can be achieved through the first and second derivatives.
- **Related Rates:** In engineering, many quantities are changing simultaneously and derivatives can help relate these changes to each other.

4. **The Integral:**
   - **Definite and Indefinite Integrals:** Integration is essentially the inverse operation of differentiation. The indefinite integral, or antiderivative, of a function is a function whose derivative is the original function. The definite integral of a function over an interval calculates the area under the curve of the function between two points.
   - **Fundamental Theorem of Calculus:** This theorem bridges the concept of differentiation and integration, providing a way to compute a definite integral via antiderivatives.

5. **Techniques of Integration:**
   - **Basic Techniques:** These include methods such as substitution and integration by parts, which are crucial for solving integrals that are not straightforward.
   - **Special Integrals:** Engineering often requires integration of trigonometric, exponential, and logarithmic functions, which have specific integration techniques.
   - **Numerical Integration:** When functions are too complex for symbolic integration, numerical methods such as the Trapezoidal Rule and Simpson's Rule are employed.

6. **Series and Approximations:**
   - **Taylor Series:** A powerful tool in calculus, the Taylor series of a function provides a polynomial approximation, which is fundamental in simulations and calculations where exact solutions are unobtainable.

Applications in Engineering

Single-variable calculus is omnipresent in engineering:

- **Mechanical Engineering:** Calculus helps in understanding the dynamics of mechanical systems under various forces.
- **Electrical Engineering:** It is used in analyzing circuits and the behavior of signals, particularly in understanding how signals change over time.
- **Civil Engineering:** Calculus is used to calculate loads and stresses in structures and to model the flow of liquids in systems.
- **Environmental Engineering:** It helps model pollutant dispersion and the flow rates in natural systems.

Conclusion

The mastery of single-variable calculus is indispensable for any aspiring engineer preparing for the FE Other Disciplines Exam. This chapter has laid out the fundamental concepts and applications of calculus in engineering, ensuring that you are well-prepared to tackle calculus-related problems in the exam and in professional practice. By understanding and applying the principles of single-variable calculus, you will enhance your ability to think critically and solve complex engineering problems efficiently.

Problems:

Problem 1: Analytic Geometry and Trigonometry
Calculate the radius of the circle defined by the equation $x^2 + y^2 - 6x + 4y = 12$.

Problem 2: Differential Equations
Solve the differential equation $\frac{dy}{dx} = 3y$ with the initial condition $y(0) = 2$.

Problem 3: Numerical Methods
Use the Trapezoidal Rule with three equal subdivisions to estimate the integral of $f(x) = x^3$ from $x = 0$ to $x = 3$.

Problem 4: Linear Algebra
Given the matrix $A = \begin{bmatrix} 2 & -1 \\ -1 & 2 \end{bmatrix}$, find the determinant.

Problem 5: Single-variable Calculus
Find the derivative of the function $f(x) = \sin(x^2)$.

Problem 6: Analytic Geometry and Trigonometry
Determine the equation of the line passing through the points (2, -3) and (4, 5).

Problem 7: Differential Equations
Find the particular solution of the differential equation $\frac{d^2y}{dx^2} - 3\frac{dy}{dx} + 2y = 12x$ given $y(0) = 0$ and $y'(0) = 1$.

Problem 8: Numerical Methods
Approximate the root of the equation $x^3 - 2x - 5 = 0$ using Newton's method starting from an initial guess of $x_0 = 2$.

Problem 9: Linear Algebra
Solve the system of linear equations:

$$3x + 4y = 5,$$
$$2x - y = 1.$$

Problem 10: Single-variable Calculus

Evaluate the integral $\int_0^1 e^{2x}\, dx$.

Solutions:

Solution 1:

The given equation is $x^2 + y^2 - 6x + 4y = 12$. Completing the square,

$$(x^2 - 6x) + (y^2 + 4y) = 12 \implies (x-3)^2 + (y+2)^2 = 25$$

The radius of the circle is 5.

Solution 2:

This is a simple first-order linear differential equation. Integrating,

$$y = Ce^{3x}.$$

Solution 3:

Using the Trapezoidal Rule,

$$\int_0^3 x^3\, dx \approx \frac{3-0}{3}\left[\frac{0^3 + 3^3}{2} + 1^3 + 2^3\right] = 1\left[\frac{0+27}{2} + 1 + 8\right] = 22.5.$$

Solution 4:

The determinant of matrix A is calculated as:

$$\det(A) = (2)(2) - (-1)(-1) = 4 - 1 = 3.$$

Solution 5:

Using the chain rule,

$$\frac{d}{dx}\sin(x^2) = \cos(x^2) \cdot 2x = 2x\cos(x^2).$$

Solution 6:

Using the point-slope form,

$$\frac{y+3}{x-2} = \frac{5+3}{4-2} = \frac{8}{2} = 4.$$

Thus, the equation is $y + 3 = 4(x - 2)$ or $y = 4x - 11$.

Solution 7:

The characteristic equation is $r^2 - 3r + 2 = 0$, with roots $r = 1, 2$. The general solution is $y = C_1 e^x + C_2 e^{2x}$. Adding the particular solution for the non-homogeneous part, $y_p = Ax$,

$$A = 6 \implies y = C_1 e^x + C_2 e^{2x} + 6x.$$

Using the initial conditions to solve for C_1 and C_2, $y(0) = 0 \implies C_1 + C_2 = 0$ and $y'(0) = 1 \implies C_1 + 2C_2 = 1$. Solving, $C_1 = 2, C_2 = -2$.

$$y = 2e^x - 2e^{2x} + 6x.$$

Solution 8:

Applying Newton's method,

$$x_{n+1} = x_n - \frac{f(x_n)}{f'(x_n)}.$$

For $f(x) = x^3 - 2x - 5$,

$$f'(x) = 3x^2 - 2.$$

Starting with $x_0 = 2$,

$$x_1 = 2 - \frac{2^3 - 2 \cdot 2 - 5}{3 \cdot 2^2 - 2} = 2 - \frac{1}{10} = 1.9.$$

Solution 9:

Using matrix methods, convert the system to an augmented matrix and perform row operations to find x and y. The solution is $x = 1$ and $y = 0.5$.

Solution 10:

The integral of e^{2x} from 0 to 1 is,

$$\int_0^1 e^{2x}\, dx = \left[\frac{1}{2}e^{2x}\right]_0^1 = \frac{1}{2}(e^2 - 1).$$

Chapter 2: Probability and Statistics

Estimation Techniques

Estimation techniques in statistics are critical for engineers and scientists to make predictions and decisions based on data samples. These techniques allow practitioners to infer the characteristics of a population from a sample, thus providing crucial insights without the need for a complete population investigation. The understanding and application of these techniques are essential in areas ranging from quality control and product reliability to environmental engineering and risk analysis.

Key Concepts in Estimation

1. Population and Sample:

- **Population:** The entire group about which information is desired.
- **Sample:** A subset of the population, selected to represent the population in statistical studies.

2. Parameter and Statistic:

- **Parameter:** A numerical characteristic of a population, such as a mean (μ) or standard deviation (σ).
- **Statistic:** A characteristic of a sample that estimates the corresponding population parameter, such as the sample mean ($\bar{x}$) or sample standard deviation (s).

Types of Estimators

1. Point Estimation: Point estimation involves the use of sample data to compute a single value (known as a point estimator) that is a best guess of an unknown population parameter. The main point estimators are:

- **Sample Mean ($\bar{x}$):** Used to estimate the population mean (μ).
- **Sample Variance (S^2):** Used to estimate the population variance (σ^2).

2. Interval Estimation: Unlike point estimation, interval estimation calculates a range (or interval) of values that is likely to contain the population parameter. This interval estimation provides a measure of uncertainty associated with the estimate. The most common interval estimates are:

- **Confidence Interval:** Provides a range of values for the population parameter. For example, a 95% confidence interval for the mean states that if the same population is sampled multiple times, approximately 95% of the intervals will contain the population mean.

Properties of Good Estimators

A good estimator should have the following properties:

- **Unbiasedness:** The expected value of the estimator should equal the true parameter value.
- **Consistency:** As the sample size increases, the estimator should converge to the true parameter value.
- **Efficiency:** Of all the unbiased estimators, an efficient estimator has the smallest variance.

- **Sufficiency:** An estimator is sufficient if it uses all the information in the sample that relates to the parameter being estimated.

Estimation Techniques and Their Application

1. Method of Moments: This method involves equating the theoretical moments (like mean and variance) of a probability distribution to the corresponding sample moments to solve for the parameters of the distribution. It's a straightforward and easy-to-understand method but might not always provide the most efficient estimator.

2. Maximum Likelihood Estimation (MLE): MLE is a method of estimating the parameters of a statistical model by maximizing a likelihood function, so the observed data is most probable under the assumed statistical model. MLEs are widely used due to their desirable properties under many conditions, such as asymptotic normality and efficiency.

Practical Application of Estimation Techniques in Engineering

- **Quality Control:** Estimation techniques are used to assess whether products meet quality standards. For example, the average tensile strength of a batch of steel cables can be estimated to determine if the batch meets specifications.

- **Environmental Engineering:** Estimators are used to predict pollutant levels from a sample of measurements to assess compliance with environmental standards.

- **Risk Analysis:** Estimators help in assessing the probability of failure in safety-critical systems, thus informing maintenance schedules and safety protocols.

Conclusion

Estimation techniques form a fundamental part of statistical inference, providing a bridge between sample data and population parameters. Mastery of these techniques enables engineers to make informed decisions based on partial data, which is often the only practical way to manage real-world uncertainties. Understanding both the theory and application of various estimation methods is crucial for the FE Other Disciplines Exam and professional practice in engineering fields. This knowledge not only aids in passing the exam but also equips engineers with the skills necessary to apply statistical methods to a wide range of problems in the engineering world.

Expected Value and Decision Making

Introduction to Expected Value and Decision Making
Expected value is a fundamental concept in probability and statistics that provides a measure of the center, or mean, of a probability distribution. It represents the average outcome one would expect after many repetitions of a random experiment. In decision making, especially in engineering and business contexts, expected value plays a crucial role in guiding decisions under uncertainty by quantifying different outcomes based on their probabilities.
Understanding Expected Value

1. Definition of Expected Value:

The expected value (EV) of a random variable is the probability-weighted average of all possible values. For a discrete random variable X with possible values $x_1, x_2, ..., x_n$ and probabilities $P(X = x_i)$, the expected value $E(X)$ is defined as:

$$E(X) = \sum_{i=1}^{n} x_i P(X = x_i)$$

For continuous random variables, the expected value is calculated using an integral over the range of all possible outcomes.

2. Properties of Expected Value:

- **Linearity:** The expected value operator is linear, which means $E(aX + bY) = aE(X) + bE(Y)$ for any two random variables X and Y, and constants a and b.
- **Additivity:** For any two random variables X and Y, $E(X + Y) = E(X) + E(Y)$.

Expected Value in Decision Making

1. Decision Analysis: In decision analysis, expected value is used to identify the best course of action when dealing with probabilistic scenarios. It involves listing all possible outcomes, determining the likelihood of each outcome, and calculating the expected value of each decision path.

2. Risk Analysis: Expected value calculations help assess the risk associated with different decisions by considering the potential gains and losses weighted by their respective probabilities. This analysis is crucial in fields such as finance, engineering, and management, where decision outcomes are uncertain.

Applications of Expected Value in Engineering

1. Engineering Economics: In engineering economics, expected value is used to calculate the probable costs and benefits of projects under different scenarios. This aids in project budgeting and financial planning, ensuring that resources are allocated efficiently and risks are minimized.

2. Quality Control: Manufacturers use expected value to determine the average outcome of production processes, which helps in assessing the overall quality and reliability of products. This is crucial in industries where high precision and reliability are required, such as aerospace and automotive sectors.

3. Reliability Engineering: Expected value is used in reliability engineering to predict the life expectancy of systems and components. By analyzing failure rates and the associated costs of different failure modes, engineers can make informed decisions about preventive maintenance and design improvements.

Calculating Expected Value: Practical Examples

Example 1: Investment Decision Suppose an engineer must choose between two investments. Investment A offers a 60% chance of earning $200 and a 40% chance of losing $50. Investment B offers a 90% chance of earning $100 and a 10% chance of losing $100. The expected values are:

$$E(A) = 0.6 \times 200 + 0.4 \times (-50) = 110$$
$$E(B) = 0.9 \times 100 + 0.1 \times (-100) = 80$$

Example 2: Equipment Purchase An engineer evaluates the purchase of a new machine, where Machine A has a 70% chance of increasing production efficiency by $30,000 and a 30% chance of incurring a $10,000 maintenance cost. The expected value calculation helps decide whether the investment justifies the risk:

$$E(MachineA) = 0.7 \times 30000 - 0.3 \times 10000 = 18000$$

The positive expected value suggests that purchasing Machine A is likely beneficial.

Conclusion

Expected value is a powerful tool in statistics that assists in rational decision-making under uncertainty. By understanding and applying the principles of expected value, engineers can optimize decision outcomes, thereby enhancing project success rates and operational efficiency. This chapter provides a deep dive into the theoretical underpinnings and practical applications of expected value, preparing candidates for both the FE exam and real-world engineering challenges.

Sampling Distributions

Sampling distributions are a fundamental concept in statistics that provide insight into the behavior of sample statistics over repeated sampling from a given population. Understanding sampling distributions is essential for performing statistical inference, as they form the basis for estimating the properties of populations and making decisions based on sample data. This knowledge is particularly critical in fields such as engineering, where decisions often rely on data from samples rather than complete populations.

Definition and Importance

1. Definition: A sampling distribution is the probability distribution of a given statistic based on a random sample. It describes how the values of the statistic vary from one sample to another.

2. Importance: Sampling distributions allow engineers to understand the variability of sample estimates, predict the range within which population parameters lie, and calculate the probabilities of different outcomes under various sampling scenarios. They provide the theoretical foundation for constructing confidence intervals and conducting hypothesis tests.

Key Components of Sampling Distributions

1. Population and Sample:

- **Population:** The complete set of items or data points from which samples are taken.
- **Sample:** A subset of the population used to make inferences about the population.

2. Statistic vs. Parameter:

- **Statistic:** A measure calculated from the sample data, such as the sample mean or sample variance.
- **Parameter:** A characteristic of the population, such as the population mean or population variance.

Central Theorem in Sampling Distributions

1. Central Limit Theorem (CLT): The Central Limit Theorem is pivotal in the study of sampling distributions. It states that for a sufficiently large sample size, the distribution of the sample mean will approximate a normal distribution, regardless of the shape of the population distribution, provided that the population has a finite variance. This theorem is crucial because it justifies the use of the normal distribution as an approximation in many statistical procedures.

- **Implication:** CLT allows engineers to use normal probability models to make inferences about sample means and sums, even when the original data are not normally distributed.

Constructing and Understanding Sampling Distributions

1. Sampling Distribution of the Mean: The sampling distribution of the sample mean ($\underline{X}$) is a common focus in engineering studies. It is characterized by:

- **Mean:** The mean of the sampling distribution of the mean is equal to the population mean (μ).
- **Standard Error (SE):** The standard deviation of the sampling distribution, known as the standard error, is given by $\sigma / \sqrt{n}$, where σ is the population standard deviation, and n is the sample size.

2. Sampling Distribution of the Proportion: In cases where the characteristic of interest is categorical, the sampling distribution of the sample proportion is studied. For a sample proportion p:

- **Mean:** Equal to the population proportion (π).
- **Standard Error:** Given by $\sqrt{\pi(1-\pi)/n}$.

Applications in Engineering

1. Quality Control: Engineers use sampling distributions to determine whether a batch of materials meets quality standards. By understanding the distribution of sample means, they can assess the probability that the quality of a batch deviates from specifications.

2. Risk Analysis: Sampling distributions are used to model uncertainties in engineering projects, such as the variability in load strength or material properties, which are crucial for safety assessments and design specifications.

3. Design of Experiments: Sampling distributions assist in designing experiments where engineers need to estimate the effects of various factors on a response variable. They help determine the required sample size to achieve desired precision in estimates of these effects.

Conclusion

Sampling distributions are an essential tool in the arsenal of an engineer. They provide the means to make probabilistic inferences about population parameters based on sample data, which is a cornerstone of statistical analysis in engineering. Understanding sampling distributions not only supports rigorous statistical testing and decision-making but also underpins the reliability and validity of conclusions drawn from data in engineering research and practice. This chapter has laid a solid foundation for FE exam candidates to grasp the implications and applications of sampling distributions in real-world engineering scenarios.

Goodness of Fit Tests

Goodness of fit tests are statistical procedures used to determine how well a statistical model fits a set of observations. These tests are essential in engineering and science for validating assumptions about the distribution of data, assessing model adequacy, and ensuring reliable statistical inference and decision-making based on the model.

Purpose and Importance

1. Purpose: The primary purpose of goodness of fit tests is to test the hypothesis that a sample derives from a population with a specific distribution. These tests are critical when the underlying distribution of the data affects the analysis, such as in reliability testing, quality control, and predictive modeling.

2. Importance: In engineering, ensuring that the data fits a particular distribution allows for more accurate predictions, optimized processes, and better risk management. Goodness of fit tests provide a quantitative way to assess model fit and are a fundamental part of model validation.

Key Concepts and Tests

1. Chi-Squared Goodness of Fit Test: One of the most widely used goodness of fit tests, the chi-squared test, is applied when you have observed categorical data and want to test how well the observed proportions match expected proportions under a specific model.

- **Test Statistic:** $x^2 = \sum \frac{(O_i - E_i)^2}{E_i}$

  where Oi are the observed frequencies, and Ei are the expected frequencies under the null hypothesis.

- **Degrees of Freedom:** Typically k−1−p, where k is the number of categories, and p is the number of parameters estimated from the data.

- **Usage:** Commonly used to test hypotheses about the distribution of categorical variables, such as the distribution of defects in manufactured products or the frequency distribution of failure modes.

2. Kolmogorov-Smirnov Test: The Kolmogorov-Smirnov (K-S) test is used to decide if a sample comes from a population with a specific distribution. It is nonparametric and measures the largest distance (D) between the empirical distribution function of the sample and the cumulative distribution function of the reference distribution.

- **Test Statistic:** $D = sup_x | F_n(x) - F(x)|$ where $F_n(x)$ is the empirical distribution function of the sample, and $F(x)$ is the cumulative distribution function of the hypothesized distribution.

- **Usage:** Useful in checking the fit of data to continuous distributions, which is particularly relevant in processes where the data must follow a specific continuous distribution for analytical models to be valid.

Applications in Engineering

1. Manufacturing: Goodness of fit tests are used to verify that the production process yields products that conform to specified quality standards. For instance, if a process is assumed to produce attributes that are normally distributed, a goodness of fit test can validate this assumption.

2. Reliability Engineering: In reliability engineering, goodness of fit tests help determine if the life of a product, such as the time to failure, follows a specific distribution like the exponential or Weibull distribution. This information is crucial for accurate reliability forecasts and maintenance planning.

3. Environmental Science: Engineers and scientists use these tests to analyze environmental data, such as the distribution of pollutant levels, to ensure compliance with environmental standards and to model environmental risks accurately.

Conducting a Goodness of Fit Test

1. Steps in Conducting the Test:

- **Step 1:** Specify the null hypothesis that the data follows a certain distribution.
- **Step 2:** Calculate the expected frequencies based on the hypothesized distribution.
- **Step 3:** Compute the observed frequencies from the sample data.
- **Step 4:** Calculate the test statistic (e.g., chi-squared or K-S statistic).
- **Step 5:** Determine the p-value or compare the test statistic to the critical value from the appropriate distribution (chi-squared or K-S) to decide whether to reject the null hypothesis.

2. Decision Making: A small p-value (typically less than 0.05) suggests that the observed data do not fit the hypothesized distribution well, leading to the rejection of the null hypothesis. Conversely, a large p-value suggests an acceptable fit.

Conclusion

Goodness of fit tests are an indispensable tool in statistical analysis, providing a methodical approach for assessing whether data adhere to a specified distribution. Mastery of these tests enables engineers to make informed decisions based on statistical models, ensuring that their conclusions and subsequent actions are grounded in data that accurately reflects the underlying assumptions of their analytical models. This knowledge not only prepares candidates for the FE exam but also equips them to tackle real-world engineering challenges with confidence.

Problems:

Problem 1: Estimation Techniques What is the point estimate of the population mean if five sample measurements are 10, 12, 14, 16, and 18?

Problem 2: Expected Value and Decision Making Calculate the expected value of a game that pays $100 with a probability of 0.2, $50 with a probability of 0.3, and loses $25 with a probability of 0.5.

Problem 3: Sampling Distributions Given a large population with a mean of 50 and a standard deviation of 10, what is the standard error of the mean for a sample size of 25?

Problem 4: Goodness of Fit Tests You observe 100 rolls of a six-sided die and record the following frequencies: 18, 16, 14, 17, 20, 15. Test if the die is fair using the chi-squared goodness of fit test at a 0.05 significance level.

Problem 5: Estimation Techniques Calculate a 95% confidence interval for the population mean if the sample mean is 30, the sample standard deviation is 5, and the sample size is 36.

Problem 6: Expected Value and Decision Making A project has a 40% chance to gain $200,000 and a 60% chance to lose $150,000. What is the expected monetary value of the project?

Problem 7: Sampling Distributions If the sampling distribution of the sample mean is normally distributed, what can be inferred about the population distribution if the sample size is large?

Problem 8: Goodness of Fit Tests Use the Kolmogorov-Smirnov test to assess if the following sample data comes from a standard normal distribution: 0.1, -1.2, 0.3, 0.5, -0.7.

Problem 9: Estimation Techniques Determine the sample variance and standard deviation for the data set: 5, 7, 9, 10, 12.

Problem 10: Expected Value and Decision Making If a stock can increase in value by $10 with a probability of 0.7 or decrease by $10 with a probability of 0.3, what is the expected change in the stock's value?

Solutions:

Solution 1:

The point estimate of the population mean is the sample mean:
$$\bar{x} = \frac{10+12+14+16+18}{5} = 14$$

Solution 2:
$$E(X) = 100 \times 0.2 + 50 \times 0.3 - 25 \times 0.5 = 20 + 15 - 12.5 = 22.5$$

Solution 3:

Using the formula for the standard error of the mean,
$$SE = \frac{\sigma}{\sqrt{n}} = \frac{10}{\sqrt{25}} = 2$$

Solution 4:

Expected frequency for each outcome (if the die is fair) is $\frac{100}{6} \approx 16.67$.

$$\chi^2 = \sum \frac{(O-E)^2}{E} = \frac{(18-16.67)^2}{16.67} + \cdots + \frac{(15-16.67)^2}{16.67} = 1.795$$

Refer to the chi-squared distribution table in the NCEES FE Reference Handbook for critical values. The degrees of freedom = 5, and for $\alpha = 0.05$, $\chi^2_{0.05,5} = 11.07$. Since $1.795 < 11.07$, do not reject the null hypothesis; the die appears fair.

Solution 5:

Confidence Interval $= \bar{x} \pm z \times \frac{s}{\sqrt{n}} = 30 \pm 1.96 \times \frac{5}{6} = [28.27, 31.73]$

Solution 6:

$E(X) = 0.4 \times 200,000 - 0.6 \times 150,000 = 80,000 - 90,000 = -10,000$

Solution 7:

If the sampling distribution of the sample mean is normally distributed and the sample size is large, the population distribution does not necessarily need to be normal due to the Central Limit Theorem.

Solution 8:

The Kolmogorov-Smirnov test would require calculating the maximum difference between the empirical and the theoretical cumulative distribution functions. This would be best performed using statistical software, as manual calculations are complex.

Solution 9:

$$s^2 = \frac{\sum(x_i - \bar{x})^2}{n-1} = \frac{(5-8.6)^2 + (7-8.6)^2 + \cdots + (12-8.6)^2}{4} = 8.3$$

$s = \sqrt{8.3} \approx 2.88$

Solution 10:

$E(X) = 10 \times 0.7 - 10 \times 0.3 = 7 - 3 = 4$

These problems and solutions provide a comprehensive review of the topics in Chapter 2, preparing candidates for the types of questions they might encounter on the FE exam while enhancing their understanding of probability and statistics in engineering contexts.

Chapter 3: Chemistry

Oxidation and Reduction

Oxidation and reduction, commonly referred to as redox reactions, are a fundamental class of chemical reactions important across a wide range of scientific disciplines, including chemistry, biology, environmental science, and engineering. These reactions are essential for processes such as energy production, metallurgy, and the functioning of batteries. Understanding redox reactions is crucial for engineers to effectively manage processes that involve electron transfer, corrosion, and energy conversion.

Basic Concepts of Oxidation and Reduction

1. Definitions:

- **Oxidation:** Refers to the loss of electrons by a molecule, atom, or ion.

- **Reduction:** Refers to the gain of electrons by a molecule, atom, or ion. The concept of oxidation and reduction can be remembered by the mnemonic "LEO the lion says GER": Lose Electrons Oxidation, Gain Electrons Reduction.

2. Oxidation Numbers: The oxidation number, or oxidation state, is a useful concept for tracking electrons during chemical reactions. It is a hypothetical charge that an atom would have if all bonds to atoms of different elements were 100% ionic. Changes in oxidation states during a reaction indicate the movement of electrons and help identify which species are oxidized and which are reduced.

The Redox Process

1. Electron Transfer: The fundamental feature of redox reactions is the transfer of electrons from one reactant to another. Oxidation and reduction always occur simultaneously, in a sense balancing each other because the electrons lost by the oxidized species are gained by the reduced species.

2. Balancing Redox Equations: Balancing redox reactions involves ensuring that both the number of atoms and the charge are balanced on both sides of the reaction equation. This can typically be done using two methods:

- **Half-Reaction Method:** Splits the overall reaction into two half-reactions, one for oxidation and one for reduction. Each half-reaction is balanced separately, and then the half-reactions are added back together.

- **Oxidation Number Method:** Changes in oxidation numbers are calculated to determine the number of electrons lost and gained, which helps balance the reaction.

Applications of Oxidation and Reduction

1. Energy Production: Redox reactions are at the heart of many energy-producing devices, such as batteries and fuel cells. In these devices, oxidation and reduction reactions occur at separate electrodes, generating electric current as electrons flow through an external circuit from the anode (where oxidation occurs) to the cathode (where reduction occurs).

2. Corrosion: Corrosion, a major issue in materials science and engineering, is essentially a redox process where metal is oxidized by substances in the environment. Understanding the electrochemistry of redox reactions allows engineers to design more effective corrosion prevention methods.

3. Metallurgy: Redox reactions are fundamental to extracting metals from ores. For example, iron is produced from iron ore primarily through the reduction of iron oxides to iron metal using carbon monoxide in a blast furnace.

4. Environmental Chemistry: Redox chemistry is crucial in environmental processes and remediation strategies. For instance, the bioremediation of contaminated sites often relies on microbial redox reactions to degrade pollutants.

Challenges in Redox Chemistry

Redox reactions can be complex due to the need to balance charge and mass in the equations. Moreover, the practical applications, such as in corrosion or battery technology, often involve intricate setups where the control of reaction conditions, like pH and temperature, is crucial.

Conclusion

Oxidation and reduction reactions form the basis of many processes in natural and industrial systems. For engineers and scientists, a thorough understanding of redox processes is essential not only for managing and optimizing these reactions but also for developing new technologies that are more efficient, sustainable, and environmentally friendly. Mastery of redox chemistry enables professionals to innovate and solve practical problems in a variety of fields, making it a vital component of education in the sciences.

Acids and Bases

Acids and bases are fundamental concepts in both chemistry and biochemistry, playing essential roles in a wide array of industrial, environmental, and biological processes. From the production of chemicals to the regulation of biochemical pathways, understanding the properties of acids and bases is crucial for engineers and scientists in designing efficient, safe, and sustainable systems.

Basic Concepts of Acids and Bases

1. Definitions and Theories:

- **Arrhenius Definition:** An acid is a substance that increases the concentration of hydrogen ions (H+) in solution, while a base increases the concentration of hydroxide ions (OH-).
- **Brønsted-Lowry Theory:** This more general theory defines acids as proton donors and bases as proton acceptors. This theory is applicable to both aqueous and non-aqueous solutions.
- **Lewis Theory:** A broader definition where acids are electron pair acceptors and bases are electron pair donors. This theory encompasses reactions that do not involve protons directly.

2. pH and pOH:

- **pH:** A measure of the acidity or alkalinity of a solution, defined as the negative logarithm (base 10) of the hydrogen ion concentration. pH values below 7 indicate acidity, values above 7 indicate alkalinity, and a pH of 7 is neutral, characteristic of pure water at 25°C.
- **pOH:** Similarly, pOH is the negative logarithm of the hydroxide ion concentration and is used alongside pH to describe the degree of acidity or basicity of a solution.

Properties of Acids and Bases

1. Chemical Properties:

- **Acids:** Taste sour, react strongly with metals, turn blue litmus paper red, and are often corrosive.
- **Bases:** Taste bitter, feel slippery, turn red litmus paper blue, and can also be corrosive.

2. Strength of Acids and Bases:

- **Strong Acids/Bases:** Dissociate completely in solution, releasing all their hydrogen or hydroxide ions, respectively. Examples include hydrochloric acid (HCl) and sodium hydroxide (NaOH).
- **Weak Acids/Bases:** Only partially dissociate in solution. An example is acetic acid (CH_3COOH), which partially dissociates to release hydrogen ions.

Balancing Acid-Base Reactions

Acid-base reactions, typically involving the transfer of protons between reactants, can be balanced by ensuring that the number of H+ ions lost by the acid equals the number of H+ ions gained by the base. This balance is crucial in stoichiometric calculations involved in the process design and quantitative analysis.

Applications of Acids and Bases

1. Industrial Applications:

- **Manufacturing:** Acids and bases are used in the manufacture of a variety of products including fertilizers, plastics, pharmaceuticals, and dyes.
- **Water Treatment:** Acids and bases play critical roles in adjusting pH levels in water treatment processes to ensure safety and effectiveness.

2. Environmental Impact:

- **Acid Rain:** Understanding the chemistry of acids is important for addressing the environmental impact of acid rain, which affects water bodies, forests, and soil chemistry.
- **Buffer Solutions:** Buffers, which are solutions that resist changes in pH, are crucial in natural water bodies and are used to manage pH in industrial processes.

3. Biological Significance:

- **Metabolism:** Enzymatic reactions often require specific pH levels for optimal activity. Acids and bases are fundamental in maintaining the homeostasis of biological fluids such as blood.
- **Nutrient Availability:** The pH of the soil affects the availability of nutrients. Acidic soils can make certain nutrients more available than others, influencing plant growth and agricultural productivity.

Challenges in Managing Acids and Bases

The management of acids and bases requires careful consideration of safety and environmental impact. Handling these substances involves risks due to their corrosive nature and potential for hazardous reactions. Moreover, the disposal of acidic or basic waste requires neutralization processes to prevent environmental damage.

Conclusion

Acids and bases are not only pivotal in numerous scientific and industrial processes but also essential for environmental management and biological functions. A deep understanding of acid-base chemistry is crucial for engineers and scientists to innovate and solve problems across various fields effectively. This chapter provides the fundamental knowledge and applications necessary for proficiency in handling acidic and basic substances, preparing professionals for both practical challenges and opportunities.

Chemical Reactions

Chemical reactions are processes where reactants are transformed into products through the breaking and forming of chemical bonds. Understanding chemical reactions is fundamental for engineers and scientists, enabling them to manipulate matter at the molecular level for a variety of applications, from energy conversion and pharmaceuticals to materials science and environmental technology.

Basic Concepts of Chemical Reactions

1. Types of Reactions:

- **Synthesis Reactions:** Two or more reactants combine to form a single product (A + B → AB).
- **Decomposition Reactions:** A compound breaks down into simpler substances (AB → A + B).
- **Single Displacement Reactions:** One element replaces another in a compound (A + BC → AC + B).
- **Double Displacement Reactions:** Ions between two compounds exchange places (AB + CD → AD + CB).
- **Combustion Reactions:** A substance reacts with oxygen, releasing energy as light and heat, typically producing carbon dioxide and water (hydrocarbons with O_2).

2. Reaction Stoichiometry: Stoichiometry involves the quantitative study of reactants and products in a chemical reaction. It is essential for calculating the amounts of substances required or produced and is based on the conservation of mass and the mole concept.

Energy Changes in Reactions

1. Exothermic and Endothermic Reactions:

- **Exothermic Reactions:** Release heat, making the surroundings warmer (e.g., combustion).
- **Endothermic Reactions:** Absorb heat, cooling the surroundings (e.g., photosynthesis).

2. Activation Energy: The energy required to initiate a reaction, representing the minimum energy barrier that must be overcome for reactants to transform into products.

Reaction Rates and Equilibrium

1. Factors Affecting Reaction Rates:

- **Concentration:** Higher concentrations generally lead to faster reactions due to increased molecular interactions.
- **Temperature:** Higher temperatures typically increase reaction rates by providing more energy to the reactant molecules.
- **Catalysts:** Substances that increase the reaction rate without being consumed; they lower the activation energy.
- **Surface Area:** Greater surface area allows more rapid interactions between reactants, increasing reaction speed.

2. Chemical Equilibrium: A state where the forward and reverse reactions occur at the same rate, resulting in no net change in the concentration of reactants and products. Understanding equilibrium is crucial for processes designed to maximize product yield.

Applications of Chemical Reactions in Engineering

1. Chemical Manufacturing: Engineers design reactors and processes that optimize the yield of desired chemical products through controlled reaction conditions, ensuring efficiency and safety.

2. Environmental Engineering: Chemical reactions are used to treat pollutants in air and water, such as converting harmful chemicals into harmless substances through chemical oxidation or reduction.

3. Energy Sector: Reactions are fundamental in energy release and storage technologies, including batteries, fuel cells, and combustion engines.

4. Material Science: Synthetic reactions are used to create new materials, such as polymers and composites, with specific properties for particular applications.

Challenges in Chemical Reactions

Managing chemical reactions involves multiple challenges:

- **Selectivity:** Achieving high selectivity for desired products while minimizing by-products.
- **Scalability:** Transferring laboratory-scale reactions to industrial-scale processes without loss of efficiency.
- **Safety:** Controlling exothermic reactions and handling reactive or toxic substances safely.
- **Environmental Impact:** Developing sustainable processes that minimize waste and environmental damage.

Conclusion

Chemical reactions are at the heart of the chemical and process industries. Mastery of the principles governing these reactions allows professionals to innovate and improve products and processes. Engineers and scientists must understand the mechanisms, conditions, and kinetics of reactions to manipulate them effectively and responsibly. This chapter equips individuals with knowledge crucial for advancing in fields as diverse as pharmaceuticals, environmental science, energy, and materials engineering, providing a foundation for both practical applications and theoretical exploration.

Problems:

Problem 1: Oxidation and Reduction
What is the oxidizing agent in the following reaction? $Cu + 2Ag^+ \rightarrow Cu^{2+} + 2Ag$

Problem 2: Acids and Bases
Calculate the pH of a 0.01 M hydrochloric acid (HCl) solution.

Problem 3: Chemical Reactions
Balance the following combustion reaction: $C_3H_8 + O_2 \rightarrow CO_2 + H_2O$

Problem 4: Oxidation and Reduction
Determine the number of electrons transferred in the following balanced redox reaction: $2Fe^{3+} + 3Mg \rightarrow 2Fe + 3Mg^{2+}$

Problem 5: Acids and Bases
What is the pOH of a solution that has a hydroxide ion concentration of $1 \times 10^{-3} M$?

Problem 6: Chemical Reactions
Identify the type of reaction: $2KClO_3 \rightarrow 2KCl + 3O_2$

Problem 7: Oxidation and Reduction
For the electrochemical cell represented by $Zn + Cu^{2+} \rightarrow Zn^{2+} + Cu$, identify the cathode reaction.

Problem 8: Acids and Bases
A 0.25 M solution of acetic acid (CH_3COOH) is 1.3% dissociated. Calculate the concentration of H^+ ions in the solution.

Problem 9: Chemical Reactions
A reaction has a rate law expressed as $Rate = k[A][B]^2$. If the concentration of B is doubled, by what factor does the reaction rate change?

Problem 10: Oxidation and Reduction
Write the half-reaction for the reduction of hydrogen peroxide (H_2O_2) in an acidic solution.

Solutions:

Solution 1:
In the reaction $Cu + 2Ag^+ \rightarrow Cu^{2+} + 2Ag$, copper (Cu) is oxidized to Cu^{2+} by losing electrons. Ag^+ is reduced to Ag by gaining those electrons. The oxidizing agent is Ag^+, as it gains electrons.

Solution 2:
Hydrochloric acid is a strong acid and dissociates completely in water. The H^+ concentration is equal to the concentration of the acid, 0.01 M.
$pH = -\log[H^+] = -\log(0.01) = 2$

Solution 3:
The balanced equation for the combustion of propane is:
$C_3H_8 + 5O_2 \rightarrow 3CO_2 + 4H_2O$

Solution 4:
In the reaction $2Fe^{3+} + 3Mg \rightarrow 2Fe + 3Mg^{2+}$, each Mg loses 2 electrons, and each Fe^{3+} gains 1 electron. Total electrons transferred are $3 \times 2 = 6$ electrons.

Solution 5:
$pOH = -\log[OH^-] = -\log(1 \times 10^{-3}) = 3$

Solution 6:
The reaction $2KClO_3 \rightarrow 2KCl + 3O_2$ is a decomposition reaction, where $KClO_3$ breaks down into simpler substances.

Solution 7:
In the cell $Zn + Cu^{2+} \rightarrow Zn^{2+} + Cu$, the cathode reaction (where reduction occurs) is $Cu^{2+} + 2e^- \rightarrow Cu$.

Solution 8:

$[H^+] = 0.25M \times 0.013 = 0.00325M$

$pH = -\log[H^+] = -\log(0.00325) \approx 2.49$

Solution 9:

According to the rate law $Rate = k[A][B]^2$, if [B] is doubled, the rate changes by a factor of $2^2 = 4$.

Solution 10:

The reduction half-reaction for H_2O_2 in an acidic solution is:

$H_2O_2 + 2H^+ + 2e^- \rightarrow 2H_2O$

Chapter 4: Instrumentation and Controls

Sensors

Sensors are critical components in both industrial and everyday applications, acting as the eyes and ears of control systems. They convert various forms of physical energy, such as heat, light, motion, and chemical signals, into electrical signals that can be measured and analyzed. Understanding different types of sensors and their operating principles is crucial for engineers who design and maintain automated systems, robotics, manufacturing processes, and environmental monitoring systems.

Types of Sensors and Their Principles

1. Temperature Sensors:

- **Thermocouples:** Consist of two different metals joined together at one end. When the junction experiences a change in temperature, a voltage is generated that can be correlated to temperature.

- **Resistance Temperature Detectors (RTDs):** Utilize materials whose electrical resistance changes with temperature, typically platinum. They are known for their accuracy and stability.

- **Thermistors:** Similar to RTDs, but use semiconductor materials that offer higher sensitivity than RTDs, albeit with a more limited temperature range.

2. Pressure Sensors:

- **Piezoelectric Sensors:** Generate an electrical charge in response to mechanical stress and are commonly used for dynamic pressure measurements, like sound or vibration.

- **Strain Gauges:** Measure the deformation of an object as a change in electrical resistance. When applied to a flexible diaphragm, they can measure pressure differences.

- **Capacitive Pressure Sensors:** Change capacitance due to the movement of a diaphragm in response to pressure changes.

3. Flow Sensors:

- **Turbine Flow Meters:** Use a turbine that rotates within the flow stream. The rotation speed is proportional to the flow velocity.

- **Thermal Mass Flow Meters:** Measure the mass flow rate of a fluid flowing through a tube by heating the fluid and measuring the temperature change.

4. Proximity and Displacement Sensors:

- **Ultrasonic Sensors:** Emit ultrasonic waves and measure the reflection time to determine the distance to nearby objects.

- **Inductive Sensors:** Detect metallic objects via magnetic fields without direct contact.

- **Capacitive Sensors:** Measure changes in capacitance between the sensor and an object to determine presence or distance.

5. Light and Radiation Sensors:

- **Photodiodes and Phototransistors:** Convert light into an electrical current, useful in systems where light intensity needs to be monitored or controlled.
- **Infrared Sensors:** Detect infrared radiation to measure heat and movement, commonly used in security systems and thermal imaging.

6. Chemical Sensors:

- **pH Electrodes:** Measure the hydrogen ion activity in solutions, indicative of acidity or alkalinity.
- **Gas Sensors:** Detect and measure concentrations of various gases, such as carbon monoxide or methane, using techniques like chemiresistors or gas chromatography.

Applications of Sensors

1. Industrial Automation: Sensors are the foundational elements of automation, used extensively to control and optimize manufacturing processes by providing real-time data for system adjustments.

2. Environmental Monitoring: Sensors detect changes in environmental parameters, including pollution levels, weather conditions, and water quality, essential for ecological assessments and regulatory compliance.

3. Healthcare: In medical devices, sensors monitor vital signs such as heart rate, blood pressure, and blood glucose levels, playing critical roles in diagnostic equipment and wearable health monitors.

4. Consumer Electronics: Used in smartphones, tablets, and other devices, sensors enhance user interaction by responding to touch, orientation, and motion.

Challenges in Sensor Technology

1. Sensor Calibration: Maintaining accuracy involves regular calibration to ensure that sensors continue to operate correctly over time and under varying environmental conditions.

2. Sensor Integration: Integrating sensors with existing systems can be challenging, requiring careful consideration of interface standards and signal compatibility.

3. Data Management: High volumes of data from sensors necessitate robust data management solutions, which include effective data collection, processing, and storage techniques.

Conclusion

Sensors transform abstract quantities into tangible data, enabling automated systems and human operators to understand and react to their environments effectively. Mastery of sensor technology is essential for engineers involved in system design, maintenance, and innovation, providing a competitive edge in rapidly evolving technological landscapes.

Data Acquisition Systems

Data Acquisition Systems (DAQ) are integral to modern engineering, serving as the backbone for collecting, analyzing, and storing data from various sources, including sensors. These systems are essential for monitoring, controlling, and optimizing industrial processes, and for research in fields ranging from environmental science to advanced manufacturing.

Core Components of Data Acquisition Systems

1. Sensors and Signal Conditioning: DAQ systems start with sensors that convert physical phenomena into measurable electrical signals. Signal conditioning is a critical first step, involving amplifying, filtering, and converting these signals from analog to digital form. This prepares the data for accurate and efficient digital processing.

2. Analog-to-Digital Converters (ADCs): ADCs are crucial for converting conditioned analog signals into digital signals that can be processed by computers. The precision and speed of ADCs impact the quality and reliability of the data acquisition system, with resolutions ranging typically from 8 to 24 bits.

3. Data Acquisition Hardware: This hardware interfaces with the sensors and the ADCs and often includes modules for different types of inputs and outputs, multiplexers for handling multiple channels, and sometimes digital-to-analog converters (DACs) for outputting analog signals.

4. Data Logging and Storage: Collected data must be stored for analysis and record-keeping. Modern DAQ systems utilize high-capacity storage with robust data management software to organize and archive large volumes of data efficiently.

5. Software: Software for DAQ systems ranges from drivers that allow hardware to communicate with operating systems, to specialized programs that enable users to configure data collection parameters, visualize data, and perform complex analysis.

Applications of Data Acquisition Systems

1. Manufacturing: In manufacturing, DAQ systems are used to monitor production lines and machinery, ensuring that equipment operates within specified parameters, enhancing efficiency and safety.

2. Environmental Monitoring: DAQ systems are deployed in environmental monitoring to track air quality, water quality, and meteorological conditions. They provide continuous data that help in understanding environmental trends and assessing compliance with regulatory standards.

3. Energy Sector: In energy production and distribution, DAQ systems monitor variables like temperature, pressure, and flow rate, crucial for optimizing the operation of power plants and managing electrical grids.

4. Research and Development: DAQ systems are fundamental tools in R&D for experiments that require precise measurements of physical phenomena over time. They enable researchers to gather accurate data necessary for developing new technologies and scientific theories.

Advantages of Modern Data Acquisition Systems

1. Scalability: Modern DAQ systems are highly scalable, capable of expanding from a few sensor inputs to thousands, making them suitable for both small-scale experiments and large industrial applications.

2. Flexibility: With modular designs, modern systems can be customized with different types of input and output modules to meet specific needs, accommodating a wide range of sensors and signal types.

3. Real-Time Processing: Advanced DAQ systems can process data in real-time, providing immediate feedback that is essential for process control and rapid decision-making.

4. Integration with IoT: Integration with the Internet of Things (IoT) allows DAQ systems to communicate with other devices over the internet, facilitating remote monitoring and control, and enabling predictive maintenance through data analytics.

Challenges in Data Acquisition

1. Data Integrity: Ensuring the accuracy and consistency of data in the presence of noise and disturbances is a persistent challenge.

2. Data Security: Protecting sensitive data from unauthorized access, especially in systems connected to networks, is critical.

3. Compatibility: Integrating new DAQ systems with existing equipment and software can require significant effort, particularly when dealing with legacy systems.

Conclusion

Data Acquisition Systems are pivotal in translating the physical world into quantifiable, actionable data, serving as a critical tool in nearly every field of engineering and science. As technology advances, the role of DAQ systems continues to grow, driven by demands for higher precision, faster processing, and more sophisticated data analysis capabilities. Understanding these systems' capabilities and limitations is essential for engineers tasked with designing and maintaining the interconnected and automated systems of the future.

Logic Diagrams:

Logic diagrams are essential tools in engineering, used to visually represent and analyze the flow of digital signals through a system's control circuits. These diagrams are crucial for designing, understanding, and troubleshooting complex electronic and electrical systems, including automated control systems, computing infrastructure, and more.

Purpose and Importance of Logic Diagrams

Logic diagrams facilitate the comprehension and communication of how control systems and circuits function at a logical level. They help engineers and technicians to:

- Understand the operational sequences of a system.
- Predict how changes in one part of a system affect the whole.
- Aid in system design and troubleshooting.
- Provide a clear documentation for system configuration and maintenance.

Key Components of Logic Diagrams

1. Symbols: Logic diagrams use standardized symbols to represent various components and their connections within a circuit. Common symbols include:

- **Gates:** Represent logical functions like AND, OR, NOT, NAND, NOR, XOR, and XNOR.
- **Inputs and Outputs:** Indicated by labeled lines or specific symbols depending on their nature (digital, analog, etc.).
- **Connectors:** Used to show the interconnection between different components and gates within the circuit.

2. Truth Tables: Accompanying logic diagrams, truth tables provide a clear, tabular representation of the logical operation performed by the circuit. They list all possible input combinations and the corresponding output for each.

Types of Logic Diagrams

1. Block Diagrams: These are the most abstract type of logic diagrams, showing the system divided into blocks connected by lines that indicate the relationship or flow of control/data between components. They are useful during the initial stages of design to outline system structure and function.

2. Circuit Diagrams: More detailed than block diagrams, circuit diagrams show the actual paths for electrical currents and signal flow through individual components. These diagrams are essential for building and troubleshooting specific parts of a system.

3. Schematic Diagrams: Schematics provide a detailed representation, including all the electrical connections between the components. They are used extensively for circuit design and maintenance.

4. Sequence Diagrams: Used primarily in software engineering and process design, sequence diagrams show how processes operate with one another over time, offering a dynamic view of system behavior.

Applications of Logic Diagrams

1. Industrial Automation: In automated manufacturing or production processes, logic diagrams are crucial for designing and maintaining systems that rely on precise sequencing and timing of operations.

2. Software Engineering: Logic diagrams help in the planning and analysis of software logic, particularly for systems that require complex decision-making and control processes based on multiple inputs.

3. Electrical Engineering: Used for designing circuits in consumer electronics, power systems, and other electrical installations, ensuring functionality and safety.

4. Telecommunications: Logic diagrams are employed to design and maintain networks that require signal processing and switching based on predefined logical rules.

Challenges in Using Logic Diagrams

1. Complexity: As systems become more complex, their logic diagrams can become challenging to read and understand, requiring highly specialized knowledge.

2. Standardization: Maintaining standardization in symbols and drawing conventions across different engineering teams and projects is crucial for effective communication and documentation.

3. Updates and Maintenance: Keeping logic diagrams updated with system changes is vital to their continued relevance in maintenance and troubleshooting but can be resource-intensive.

Conclusion

Logic diagrams are invaluable in the field of engineering, providing a clear and structured way to visualize and understand the logical functions of control systems and circuits. Mastery of reading and creating logic diagrams enhances an engineer's ability to design, analyze, and troubleshoot systems efficiently and accurately. As technology advances, the ability to adapt and detail these diagrams becomes even more critical in the development of complex automated and digital systems.

Problems:

Problem 1: Sensors Identify the type of sensor suitable for measuring high temperatures in an industrial furnace.

Problem 2: Data Acquisition Systems What is the main function of an analog-to-digital converter in a data acquisition system?

Problem 3: Logic Diagrams What logic gate outputs high only when all its inputs are high?

Problem 4: Sensors Describe a practical application of ultrasonic sensors in automotive technology.

Problem 5: Data Acquisition Systems Explain the role of signal conditioning in a data acquisition system.

Problem 6: Logic Diagrams If an OR gate has three inputs (A, B, C) and A = 0, B = 1, C = 1, what is the output?

Problem 7: Sensors What type of sensor would be most appropriate for detecting the concentration of CO_2 in the air?

Problem 8: Data Acquisition Systems How does the sampling rate of a data acquisition system affect the quality of the acquired data?

Problem 9: Logic Diagrams Draw a simple logic diagram using AND, OR, and NOT gates to implement the function (A AND B) OR (NOT C).

Problem 10: Sensors What is the principle of operation of a capacitive proximity sensor?

Solutions:

Solution 1: Thermocouples are suitable for measuring high temperatures in industrial furnaces due to their ability to withstand extreme environments and provide accurate temperature measurements across a wide range.

Solution 2: An analog-to-digital converter (ADC) in a data acquisition system converts the analog signals received from sensors into digital signals that can be processed, analyzed, and stored by digital systems.

Solution 3: An AND gate outputs high only when all its inputs are high.

Solution 4: Ultrasonic sensors are used in automotive technology for parking assistance; they measure the distance to nearby objects and provide feedback to the driver, helping to avoid collisions.

Solution 5: Signal conditioning in a data acquisition system involves preparing sensor outputs for further processing. This includes amplification, filtering, and converting signals to forms suitable for analog-to-digital conversion, ensuring that the signals are clean and within the dynamic range of the ADC.

Solution 6: The output of an OR gate with inputs A = 0, B = 1, and C = 1 is high (1), as the OR gate outputs high if at least one input is high.

Solution 7: An infrared gas sensor would be appropriate for detecting the concentration of CO_2 in the air, as it can accurately measure gas concentrations based on infrared absorption characteristics of CO_2.

Solution 8: The sampling rate affects the quality of acquired data by determining how frequently the data acquisition system samples the input signal. A higher sampling rate provides a more accurate representation of the signal, reducing the risk of aliasing and ensuring that rapid changes in the signal are captured.

Solution 9: A simple logic diagram for the function (A AND B) OR (NOT C) would involve:

1. Connecting inputs A and B to an AND gate.
2. Connecting input C to a NOT gate.
3. Connecting the output of the AND gate and the output of the NOT gate to an OR gate.
4. The output of the OR gate represents the final output.

Solution 10: A capacitive proximity sensor operates on the principle of capacitance change. It detects objects by sensing changes in the capacitance between the sensor and the object, which varies depending on the distance and material properties of the object.

Chapter 5: Engineering Ethics and Societal Impacts

Codes of Ethics

Codes of ethics in engineering are formal guidelines that define the ethical standards and responsibilities of engineers. These codes provide a framework for professional behavior and decision-making, emphasizing integrity, honesty, fairness, and respect. They are crucial in maintaining public trust and ensuring that engineering practices contribute positively to society.

Purpose of Codes of Ethics

1. Guiding Professional Behavior: Codes of ethics serve to guide engineers in their professional conduct, ensuring that they perform their duties with the highest level of integrity and responsibility.

2. Protecting Public Safety: A primary focus of engineering ethics is the protection of public safety and welfare. Engineers are often responsible for projects that directly impact public health and safety, making ethical guidelines vital.

3. Fostering Trust: By adhering to established ethical standards, engineers help to foster trust among the public, clients, and their peers within the industry.

4. Enhancing Professionalism: Ethical guidelines promote professionalism within the engineering community, encouraging continuous improvement and learning.

Fundamental Principles in Codes of Ethics

1. Public Welfare: Engineers are expected to hold the safety, health, and welfare of the public as their paramount responsibility. This involves making decisions that protect and enhance public well-being, even if it conflicts with client or personal interests.

2. Honesty and Integrity: Engineers must perform their duties honestly and impartially, avoiding deceptive acts and clearly disclosing any conflicts of interest. This includes being truthful about one's qualifications and the potential impacts of their projects.

3. Competence: Engineers should only undertake tasks in areas of their competence and should keep their skills updated through lifelong learning. They should also provide opportunities for the professional development of their colleagues and subordinates.

4. Accountability and Transparency: Maintaining transparency in engineering decisions and accepting responsibility for one's actions are key tenets. This involves documenting decision-making processes and accepting accountability for the outcomes.

Key Codes of Ethics Examples

1. National Society of Professional Engineers (NSPE): The NSPE Code of Ethics is a benchmark in the U.S. engineering profession, emphasizing obligations to society, the environment, and upholding the integrity of the profession.

2. The Institution of Civil Engineers (ICE): The ICE promotes ethics that require engineers to strive for sustainability and to act as faithful agents or trustees of their clients and employers.

3. The Institute of Electrical and Electronics Engineers (IEEE): The IEEE Code of Ethics includes provisions for avoiding real or perceived conflicts of interest and ensuring that public comments on technical matters are made in an objective and truthful manner.

Application of Codes of Ethics in Engineering Practices

1. Environmental Considerations: Engineers must consider the environmental impact of their projects and strive for sustainable development, aligning with ethical guidelines that promote environmental stewardship.

2. Infrastructure Development: In designing and implementing infrastructure projects, engineers must ensure that the structures are safe, reliable, and capable of serving the intended purpose without adverse effects on the community or environment.

3. Technological Innovation: Ethical standards guide engineers in the responsible development and deployment of new technologies, ensuring that innovations benefit society without compromising ethical values or public welfare.

Challenges in Upholding Codes of Ethics

1. Global Differences: With engineering projects often crossing international borders, engineers face the challenge of adhering to ethical standards that may vary significantly between different countries or regions.

2. Rapid Technological Changes: Keeping ethical codes up-to-date with rapidly evolving technologies can be challenging, as new situations and dilemmas arise that may not be adequately addressed by existing guidelines.

3. Conflict of Interest: Engineers often navigate complex landscapes where the interests of different stakeholders must be balanced, making it difficult to uphold ethical principles without compromise.

Conclusion

Codes of ethics in engineering are not just guidelines but foundational elements that uphold the dignity and responsibility of the profession. They ensure that engineers act with integrity and consideration for the public good, maintaining the trust that society places in their skills and judgments. As the field of engineering evolves, so too must the ethical frameworks that guide it, ensuring that they remain relevant and effective in promoting the welfare of all.

Public Protection Issues

Public protection is a fundamental aspect of engineering ethics, focusing on the responsibility engineers have to safeguard the health, safety, and welfare of the public through their professional practices. This commitment transcends mere compliance with laws and regulations, requiring engineers to proactively anticipate, identify, and mitigate risks associated with engineering activities and decisions.

The Importance of Public Protection

The primary role of engineers is to enhance societal well-being through advancements in technology and infrastructure. However, their work often involves significant risks that can impact communities and ecosystems. The focus on public protection ensures that these risks are managed and minimized, maintaining public trust in the engineering profession.

Key Principles in Public Protection

1. Risk Assessment: Engineers must perform thorough risk assessments for projects, considering both the likelihood of adverse events and their potential impacts. This involves evaluating all phases of project development—from planning and design to construction and operation.

2. Safety and Reliability: Engineering designs and processes must prioritize safety and reliability to prevent accidents and failures that could harm the public. This includes adhering to best practices and standards that enhance the safety features of products and infrastructure.

3. Emergency Preparedness: Engineers should incorporate strategies for emergency response and disaster recovery in their projects. This includes designing infrastructure and systems that can withstand unexpected events like natural disasters or technical failures.

4. Environmental Stewardship: Public protection also involves safeguarding the environment from harmful impacts of engineering activities. Engineers must ensure that their projects comply with environmental regulations and aim for sustainability, reducing pollution and conserving resources.

Regulations and Standards for Public Protection

1. Government Regulations: Most countries have regulations that govern engineering practices to protect public health and safety. Engineers must be familiar with these regulations and ensure all projects comply with them.

2. Professional Standards: Various engineering societies and organizations establish professional standards that provide guidelines on best practices and ethical considerations. Engineers are obliged to adhere to these standards to maintain licensure and professional certification.

3. Codes of Conduct: Many engineering firms and public agencies have internal codes of conduct that outline expected behaviors and practices to protect the public. These codes often extend beyond legal requirements, emphasizing ethical responsibilities.

Case Studies and Examples

1. Building and Infrastructure Safety: The collapse of the Morandi Bridge in Italy serves as a stark reminder of the consequences of neglecting infrastructure maintenance and risk assessment, emphasizing the need for continuous monitoring and updating of engineering standards.

2. Automotive Safety Regulations: The implementation of strict safety standards in automotive design, such as mandatory airbags, anti-lock braking systems, and crash testing, illustrates how engineering responds to public safety demands.

3. Environmental Protection: The Flint water crisis highlighted the critical role engineers play in ensuring environmental safety. Failures to treat water properly to prevent pipe corrosion led to widespread lead contamination, underscoring the need for rigorous environmental oversight and ethical vigilance.

Challenges in Ensuring Public Protection

1. Balancing Cost and Safety: Engineers often face pressure to reduce costs, which can conflict with the need to allocate resources for safety measures and environmental protection.

2. Technological Complexity: As technology advances, the complexity of engineering systems increases, making it more challenging to predict and mitigate potential risks.

3. Global Standards Variation: Differing safety and environmental standards across countries can complicate multinational engineering projects, requiring engineers to navigate a complex web of regulations.

Conclusion

Public protection is a cornerstone of engineering ethics, requiring engineers to integrate safety, reliability, and environmental stewardship into every aspect of their professional duties. By rigorously applying principles of risk assessment, adhering to regulations and standards, and fostering a culture of ethical responsibility, engineers uphold their pledge to protect the public and enhance the quality of life for all members of society. This commitment not only safeguards the public but also strengthens the integrity and reputation of the engineering profession worldwide.

Societal Impacts of Engineering Decisions

Engineering decisions have far-reaching impacts on society, affecting everything from the daily lives of individuals to the global environment. The responsibility of engineers extends beyond technical and economic considerations to include social, environmental, and ethical implications. Understanding these impacts is crucial for making decisions that promote sustainability, equity, and quality of life.

The Scope of Societal Impact

1. Long-term and Wide-ranging Effects: Engineering projects can have enduring effects, both positive and negative, spanning generations. The construction of infrastructure like dams, highways, and industrial plants can shape economic opportunities, community development, and environmental conditions over time.

2. Public Welfare: Engineers must ensure their projects do not endanger public health or safety and that they enhance public welfare whenever possible. This includes considerations of accessibility, community disruption, and potential hazards.

Key Areas of Societal Impact

1. Environmental Sustainability: Engineering decisions directly influence environmental sustainability. Decisions in areas such as energy production, waste management, and material selection can mitigate or exacerbate environmental degradation.

2. Economic Development: Engineers contribute to economic development by designing and implementing technologies and infrastructure that enable commerce, improve efficiency, and create jobs. However, the economic benefits must be balanced against costs and potential socioeconomic inequalities.

3. Social Equity: Engineering projects should promote social equity by ensuring that benefits and burdens are distributed fairly across different societal groups. This includes addressing the needs of marginalized and vulnerable populations.

4. Cultural Impact: Engineering decisions can affect cultural heritage and practices, particularly when projects involve significant land use or natural resource management. Respecting cultural sites and traditions is a critical consideration.

Principles for Addressing Societal Impacts

1. Inclusivity in Planning and Design: Involving a diverse range of stakeholders in the planning and design phases of projects can help address different perspectives and needs, leading to more equitable and effective outcomes.

2. Transparency and Accountability: Maintaining transparency about potential impacts and decision-making processes builds public trust and enhances the legitimacy of engineering projects. Accountability mechanisms should be in place to address any adverse outcomes.

3. Proactive Impact Assessment: Conducting thorough impact assessments before project implementation helps identify potential negative effects on society and the environment, allowing for mitigation strategies to be developed.

Challenges in Assessing Societal Impacts

1. Complexity of Impact Analysis: The interconnected nature of modern societies makes it challenging to predict all the consequences of engineering decisions. Unintended consequences can arise from even well-planned projects.

2. Balancing Diverse Interests: Engineers often face the challenge of balancing the interests of different stakeholders, which can be conflicting. Finding compromises that align with ethical guidelines and societal needs is complex.

3. Evolving Technological and Social Contexts: As technology and societal values evolve, so too do the frameworks within which engineering decisions are made. Keeping pace with these changes requires continuous learning and adaptation.

Case Studies

1. The High-Speed Rail Projects: High-speed rail projects in various countries have reshaped economies and communities. While providing efficient transportation options, these projects also raise issues related to land use, displacement of communities, and environmental impacts.

2. Water Management Systems: Decisions in water management, such as dam construction or river diversion, have profound effects on local ecosystems, agricultural practices, and water rights. Balancing human needs with environmental sustainability is a key challenge.

Conclusion

The societal impacts of engineering decisions are profound and multifaceted. Engineers must navigate these complexities with a commitment to ethical principles, societal well-being, and environmental stewardship. By integrating considerations of public welfare, sustainability, and equity into their decision-making processes, engineers can ensure that their projects contribute positively to society and leave a beneficial legacy for future generations. This approach not only fulfills the ethical obligations of the profession but also enhances the overall quality and acceptance of engineering projects.

Problems:

Problem 1: Codes of Ethics What should an engineer do if they discover that safety tests for a new product were not conducted as specified by the industry standards?

Problem 2: Public Protection Issues An engineer finds that the material supplied for a bridge construction is substandard and could potentially jeopardize public safety. What is the first step they should take?

Problem 3: Societal Impacts of Engineering Decisions How should an engineer address concerns about a project that could significantly impact the local wildlife?

Problem 4: Codes of Ethics If an engineer is offered a gift from a contractor as a thank you for selecting their bid, what is the ethical response?

Problem 5: Public Protection Issues What is the engineer's responsibility if they notice a fellow engineer engaging in fraudulent practices?

Problem 6: Societal Impacts of Engineering Decisions How can engineers ensure that their projects promote social equity?

Problem 7: Codes of Ethics How should an engineer proceed when asked to endorse a project that is outside their area of competence?

Problem 8: Public Protection Issues What actions should an engineer take if they discover an error in their project design that has been implemented and poses a risk to the public?

Problem 9: Societal Impacts of Engineering Decisions What should an engineer consider when designing a facility in a culturally sensitive area?

Problem 10: Codes of Ethics What are the ethical implications of an engineer manipulating project data to meet the expectations of a client?

Solutions:

Solution 1: The engineer should report the issue to their supervisor or the responsible authority within the company and ensure that all safety tests comply with industry standards before proceeding further.

Solution 2: The engineer should immediately inform their project manager and document the issue. They should recommend halting the construction until the material can be replaced with one that meets the required standards.

Solution 3: The engineer should conduct an environmental impact assessment and engage with local wildlife experts and regulatory bodies to develop mitigation strategies that minimize the impact.

Solution 4: The ethical response is to decline the gift. Accepting it could compromise the engineer's impartiality or appear to do so, which violates professional ethics codes.

Solution 5: The engineer has a duty to report the fraudulent practices to appropriate authorities or their professional body, ensuring that the misconduct is addressed to protect public safety and maintain the integrity of the profession.

Solution 6: Engineers can promote social equity by involving community stakeholders in the planning process, ensuring access to the benefits of the project is not restricted, and assessing the impact of their projects on all community segments.

Solution 7: The engineer should decline to endorse the project and recommend that a qualified professional in that specific area be consulted. Providing an endorsement outside of one's expertise is unethical and can lead to misinformed decisions that may jeopardize safety or effectiveness.

Solution 8: The engineer must promptly inform their employer, the client, and any relevant regulatory bodies. They should work to rectify the error immediately to prevent potential harm.

Solution 9: The engineer should conduct thorough cultural impact studies, consult with local communities, and work closely with cultural experts to ensure the project respects local traditions and heritage.

Solution 10: Manipulating data to satisfy a client is unethical as it can lead to unsafe, unreliable, or non-optimal solutions. Such actions can endanger the public, damage the engineer's and their firm's reputation, and may have legal consequences.

Chapter 6: Safety, Health, and Environment

Industrial Hygiene

Industrial hygiene is the science of anticipating, recognizing, evaluating, and controlling workplace conditions that may cause workers' injury or illness. Industrial hygienists use environmental monitoring and analytical methods to detect the extent of worker exposure and employ engineering, work practice controls, and other methods to control potential health hazards.

The Importance of Industrial Hygiene

The primary goal of industrial hygiene is to protect and enhance the health and safety of workers, ensuring that all employment conditions contribute to workplace wellness. This discipline plays a critical role in preventing occupational diseases and accidents by controlling health hazards inherent in workplace processes.

Core Components of Industrial Hygiene

1. Anticipation and Recognition of Hazards: Industrial hygiene begins with an understanding of the potential hazards in the workplace, which can include chemical, physical, biological, and ergonomic risks. Proper training and awareness are crucial for workers and managers to recognize these hazards before they cause harm.

2. Evaluation of Hazards: This involves assessing the magnitude and significance of exposure to hazards. Industrial hygienists perform quantitative and qualitative assessments to determine the risks associated with various hazards, utilizing tools and methods such as air sampling, bio-monitoring, and noise measurement.

3. Control of Hazards: Once hazards have been identified and assessed, appropriate controls are implemented to minimize worker exposure. Controls follow a hierarchy of effectiveness:

- **Elimination:** Physically removing the hazard.
- **Substitution:** Replacing hazardous materials or processes with safer ones.
- **Engineering Controls:** Isolating workers from hazards through physical changes to the workplace.
- **Administrative Controls:** Changing work procedures or schedules to reduce exposure.
- **Personal Protective Equipment (PPE):** Using gear to protect workers when other controls are insufficient.

Applications of Industrial Hygiene

1. Chemical Hazards: Managing chemical hazards involves understanding the properties of chemicals used in the workplace and implementing proper storage, handling, and disposal practices. Exposure assessments are critical, particularly for volatile organic compounds, acids, and other hazardous chemicals.

2. Physical Hazards: Noise, radiation, and extreme temperatures are common physical hazards. Industrial hygienists work to minimize these risks by implementing soundproofing materials, radiation shields, and climate control systems.

3. Biological Hazards: In workplaces like hospitals and research facilities, workers may be exposed to biological hazards such as bacteria, viruses, and fungi. Ensuring proper sterilization, ventilation, and infection control measures are part of an industrial hygienist's duties.

4. Ergonomic Hazards: Poor ergonomic practices can lead to musculoskeletal injuries. Industrial hygienists assess work environments and redesign workstations, tools, and workflows to accommodate workers' ergonomic needs, thus reducing strain and preventing injuries.

Challenges in Industrial Hygiene

1. Rapid Technological Changes: As new technologies and materials are continuously developed, industrial hygienists must stay informed about emerging hazards and control technologies.

2. Regulatory Compliance: Maintaining compliance with local, national, and international health and safety regulations is a constant challenge due to varying and evolving standards.

3. Worker Education and Training: Educating workers about the hazards in their environment and training them to use protective equipment and practices effectively is essential but can be difficult due to language barriers, high worker turnover, and varying educational backgrounds.

Conclusion

Industrial hygiene is a crucial field within occupational health and safety, dedicated to creating safer workplaces by managing health hazards. Through a combination of science, engineering, and management principles, industrial hygienists protect workers' health and contribute to the overall productivity and morale of the workforce. Their work not only prevents illness and injury but also profoundly impacts the operational success of their organizations by fostering a healthy, safe, and compliant workplace environment.

Safety Equipment

Safety equipment, also known as personal protective equipment (PPE), plays a crucial role in minimizing exposure to hazards that cause serious workplace injuries and illnesses. The equipment protects employees from physical, chemical, electrical, mechanical, and other workplace hazards. Proper use of safety equipment is a fundamental aspect of industrial hygiene and a core responsibility for both employers and employees to ensure a safe working environment.

Types of Safety Equipment

1. Head Protection:

- **Hard Hats:** Protect against impacts from falling or flying objects, and against shocks from electrical hazards. Styles vary according to the level of protection required for specific job environments.

2. Eye and Face Protection:

- **Safety Glasses and Goggles:** Shield the eyes from flying debris, chemicals, or harmful radiation. Specialized versions are available for tasks involving lasers, welding, or exposure to intense light.

- **Face Shields:** Provide additional protection against exposure to chemical splashes and welding light when used in conjunction with primary eye protection.

3. Hearing Protection:

- **Earplugs and Earmuffs:** Used in environments with hazardous noise levels, these devices reduce noise exposure to levels that are not harmful to hearing. Selection between earmuffs and earplugs depends on the noise level, comfort, and suitability for the environment.

4. Respiratory Protection:

- **Respirators:** Range from disposable masks to full-face respirators with cartridges that filter out harmful dusts, fogs, smokes, mists, gases, vapors, and sprays. These are crucial in environments where air quality cannot be controlled by ventilation or other engineering methods.

5. Hand and Skin Protection:

- **Gloves:** Vary widely depending on the application, from disposable latex gloves to heavy-duty gloves designed to resist cuts or abrasions and to protect against chemical or thermal burns.
- **Protective Clothing:** Includes lab coats, coveralls, vests, jackets, aprons, and full body suits, tailored to protect against specific hazards like heat, chemicals, or biohazards.

6. Foot Protection:

- **Safety Shoes and Boots:** Equip with special soles to prevent slipping, puncture-resistant materials to protect from sharp objects, and insulated forms to safeguard against electrical hazards or extreme temperatures.

Importance of Safety Equipment

Safety equipment is designed to:

- **Prevent accidents and injuries:** Properly designed and used PPE can significantly reduce the risk of accidents and injuries in the workplace.
- **Reduce the severity of injuries:** In the event of an accident, safety equipment can lessen the impact of an injury, potentially saving lives and reducing the severity of harm.
- **Promote a culture of safety:** The regular use of safety equipment emphasizes the importance of safety in the workplace, encouraging all employees to adhere to safety protocols and regulations.

Challenges in the Effective Use of Safety Equipment

1. Compliance and Proper Usage: Ensuring that all workers consistently wear and correctly use PPE is a challenge. Continuous training and monitoring are necessary to maintain high levels of compliance.

2. Selection and Maintenance: Choosing the correct type of safety equipment for specific hazards and maintaining this equipment in a functional and sanitary condition are essential for effective protection.

3. Comfort and Fit: PPE must be comfortable and well-fitting to ensure that workers will wear it consistently. Discomfort and poor fit can lead to non-compliance.

Conclusion

Safety equipment is a fundamental element of risk control in the workplace, essential for protecting employees from a wide array of occupational hazards. Its effective use requires careful selection, regular maintenance, and ongoing training to ensure it is used properly and consistently. By integrating safety equipment protocols into their safety management systems, organizations can not only comply with legal requirements but also significantly enhance the well-being and productivity of their workforce.

Gas Detection and Monitoring

Gas detection and monitoring systems are essential tools in ensuring workplace safety, particularly in industries where toxic or combustible gases are present. These systems are designed to detect the presence of dangerous gases before they reach harmful concentrations, allowing for timely evacuation and response to prevent accidents, health issues, and fatalities.

Importance of Gas Detection and Monitoring

The primary function of gas detection systems is to protect life and property by providing early warnings of hazardous conditions. Effective gas monitoring can prevent explosions, fires, and exposure to toxic substances, which are critical in maintaining a safe working environment and complying with occupational health and safety regulations.

Types of Gas Detectors

1. Catalytic Sensors:

- Used for detecting combustible gases. They operate by oxidizing the gas on a catalytic surface, which changes the temperature and alters an electrical resistance.

2. Infrared (IR) Sensors:

- Utilize IR light to detect gases by the absorption characteristics specific to different gases. These are particularly useful in environments where poisons might deactivate catalytic sensors.

3. Electrochemical Sensors:

- Measure the concentration of a particular gas through an electrochemical reaction that generates a current proportional to the amount of gas present. These sensors are highly sensitive and are commonly used for detecting toxic gases at low concentrations.

4. Semiconductor Sensors:

- Use a semiconductor material to detect gases through changes in resistance when a gas interacts with the surface. These are typically used for detecting a broad range of toxic gases.

5. Photoionization Detectors (PID):

- Detect volatile organic compounds (VOCs) and other toxic gases by ionizing the gas with ultraviolet light and measuring the resulting current.

Applications of Gas Detection Systems

1. **Industrial Applications:**

    - In industries such as petrochemical, manufacturing, and mining, gas detectors are crucial for detecting explosive and toxic gases like methane, hydrogen sulfide, and carbon monoxide.

2. **Environmental Monitoring:**

    - Gas detectors are used to monitor emissions and environmental contaminants, aiding in compliance with environmental protection standards.

3. **Public Safety:**

    - Used in public facilities such as airports, malls, and office buildings to detect refrigerant leaks or carbon monoxide buildup.

4. **Confined Spaces:**

    - Essential in confined space applications where lack of ventilation can lead to hazardous accumulations of gases, necessitating rigorous monitoring for the safety of workers.

Challenges in Gas Detection

1. **Sensor Sensitivity and Selectivity:**

    - Maintaining high sensitivity to low levels of gases while ensuring selectivity against non-target gases is a significant challenge, particularly in environments with a complex mixture of chemical substances.

2. **Environmental Interference:**

    - Changes in temperature, humidity, and presence of other chemicals can affect the accuracy of gas sensors, requiring frequent calibration and maintenance to ensure reliability.

3. **Implementation and Maintenance Costs:**

    - High-quality gas detection systems are often costly to install and maintain, but necessary for compliance with safety standards.

Innovations in Gas Detection Technology

1. **Wireless and IoT-Enabled Detectors:**

    - The integration of wireless technology allows for real-time monitoring and data analytics across complex industrial sites, improving the speed and accuracy of responses to gas leaks.

2. **Smart Sensors:**

    - Advanced sensors equipped with onboard diagnostics and networking capabilities that facilitate easier maintenance, calibration, and improved reliability.

3. **Portable and Wearable Detectors:**

    - Development of small, portable, or wearable detectors enhances personal safety by providing individual monitoring in varying work environments.

Conclusion

Gas detection and monitoring is a vital component of industrial safety, protecting workers from potentially life-threatening exposures and contributing to the overall safety culture within hazardous work environments. As technology advances, these systems are becoming more sophisticated, offering greater accuracy, reliability, and integration capabilities, ultimately enhancing their ability to safeguard health and property effectively.

Electrical Safety

Electrical safety is a critical aspect of occupational safety, focusing on the prevention of electrical hazards that could lead to injuries, fatalities, and property damage. This discipline encompasses a broad range of practices and regulations designed to ensure safe installations, operations, and maintenance of electrical systems and equipment.

Importance of Electrical Safety

The significance of electrical safety stems from the inherent dangers associated with electricity, such as electric shock, electrical burns, and the potential for fires or explosions caused by faulty electrical systems. Effective electrical safety measures are essential to protect workers, especially in industries involving high-voltage systems, electronics manufacturing, and energy production.

Core Principles of Electrical Safety

1. Understanding Electrical Hazards:

- **Shock and Electrocution:** Occurs when a person comes into contact with an energized part, allowing current to flow through the body.

- **Arc Flash and Blast:** An arc flash is a dangerous condition associated with the release of energy caused by an electric arc. This phenomenon can result in severe burns, hearing loss, and eye injuries.

- **Fire and Explosion:** Faulty wiring, overloaded circuits, and poor maintenance can lead to fires and explosions, which are hazardous not only to workers but also to the environment.

2. Risk Assessment and Management: Conducting thorough risk assessments to identify potential electrical hazards and implementing appropriate risk management strategies are foundational elements of electrical safety. This involves regular inspections, system analyses, and adherence to best practices and safety standards.

Electrical Safety Measures

1. Grounding and Bonding: Proper grounding and bonding of electrical systems help to prevent buildup of voltages that could lead to electrical shock or fires.

2. Circuit Protection Devices:

- **Fuses and Circuit Breakers:** Automatically cut off electrical power in cases of overload or short circuit, protecting against wire damage and fires.

- **Ground Fault Circuit Interrupters (GFCIs):** Protect individuals from electric shock by interrupting a circuit when an imbalance between incoming and outgoing current occurs.

3. **Personal Protective Equipment (PPE):**

- **Insulating Gloves and Tools:** Provide protection against electrical shocks and burns.
- **Arc Flash Protective Clothing:** Shields against the thermal effects of arc blasts, which can reach extremely high temperatures.

4. **Lockout/Tagout Procedures:** These procedures ensure that electrical equipment is properly shut off and inoperable while maintenance or repair work is being done, preventing accidental energization.

Training and Awareness

1. **Employee Training Programs:** Training is crucial for any worker who might come into contact with electrical systems. Programs should cover the basics of electrical safety, emergency response, and the proper use of PPE.

2. **Safety Signage and Labeling:** Clear labeling and signage are essential to warn about potential electrical hazards and guide workers in following safe practices.

Challenges in Electrical Safety

1. **Compliance with Standards:** Keeping up-to-date with national and international safety standards (like those from the National Fire Protection Association, NFPA) is necessary but can be challenging due to frequent updates and revisions.

2. **Technological Advancements:** As technology evolves, new electrical safety challenges arise, requiring ongoing education and adaptation of safety practices.

3. **Human Factors:** Human error remains one of the most significant challenges in electrical safety. Continuous efforts to improve safety culture and encourage vigilance are necessary.

Conclusion

Electrical safety is a complex but essential area of workplace safety that requires rigorous standards, continuous training, and proper equipment and procedures. By implementing comprehensive safety measures and fostering a culture of safety, organizations can significantly reduce the risks associated with electrical work and enhance the overall safety and productivity of their operations.

Confined Space Entry

Confined space entry involves working in enclosed or partially enclosed spaces that are not designed for continuous occupancy and are difficult to enter or exit. These spaces can include tanks, vessels, silos, storage bins, hoppers, vaults, and pits. Confined spaces are particularly dangerous due to their restrictive nature and the potential presence of hazardous substances or dangerous conditions.

Importance of Confined Space Safety

Safety in confined spaces is critical due to the high risk of suffocation, poisoning, fires, explosions, and other serious injuries or fatalities. The hazards associated with confined spaces are often intensified by the limited access and egress, making emergency responses more challenging. Effective management of confined space entry is essential to ensure worker safety and compliance with occupational health and safety regulations.

Core Principles of Confined Space Entry

1. Hazard Identification: Before entering a confined space, it is crucial to identify potential hazards. These can include toxic atmospheres, oxygen deficiency, flammable environments, and physical hazards such as entrapment or engulfment.

2. Risk Assessment: Evaluating the risks associated with entering a confined space involves considering the nature of the work to be done, the environmental conditions inside the space, and the potential for sudden changes in those conditions.

3. Atmosphere Testing and Monitoring: Continuous atmospheric testing is necessary to detect toxic gases, flammable gases, and to ensure adequate oxygen levels. Monitoring must be performed before and during entry to ensure that the environment remains safe.

Procedures and Equipment for Safe Entry

1. Entry Permits: A confined space entry permit is required for each entry into a designated confined space. The permit system ensures that all safety measures are in place before entry and that the entry is justified. It typically includes information on the purpose of entry, the duration, the personnel involved, and the specific hazards and controls.

2. Ventilation: Proper ventilation is essential to maintain a safe working environment within confined spaces. Mechanical ventilation helps to control atmospheric hazards by ensuring a fresh air supply and removing contaminated air.

3. Personal Protective Equipment (PPE): Depending on the hazards identified, suitable PPE may include respiratory protection, protective clothing, and equipment designed to protect against specific chemical or physical hazards.

4. Communication Systems: Reliable communication systems are vital for workers inside confined spaces to maintain contact with attendants or rescue personnel outside. These systems can include radios, signals, or pull lines.

5. Rescue and Emergency Equipment: Equipment for rescue operations should be readily available at the site of confined space work. This includes harnesses, retrieval lines, and respiratory apparatus that can be used to extract workers quickly and safely if an emergency arises.

6. Training and Drills: All personnel involved in confined space entry must receive comprehensive training on the potential hazards, emergency procedures, and use of necessary equipment. Regular drills should be conducted to ensure that emergency procedures are effective and well understood.

Challenges in Confined Space Safety

1. Changing Conditions: Conditions within a confined space can change rapidly, such as sudden releases of gases or changes in oxygen levels, which can quickly turn a safe environment into a lethal one.

2. Compliance and Enforcement: Ensuring compliance with safety standards and regulations is challenging but essential. Regular audits and inspections are necessary to enforce policies and procedures.

3. Psychological Factors: Working in confined spaces can be psychologically demanding. Claustrophobia and panic attacks are risks that need to be managed both in terms of selecting personnel and providing psychological support.

Conclusion

Safety in confined spaces is a complex aspect of workplace safety, requiring meticulous planning, robust procedures, and comprehensive training. By adhering to stringent safety standards and continuously enhancing safety practices, organizations can protect their employees from the unique and significant risks associated with confined space entry. This proactive approach not only saves lives but also fosters a culture of safety and vigilance that permeates all aspects of industrial operations.

Hazard Communications

Hazard communication, commonly referred to as HazCom, is a critical aspect of workplace safety that involves the proper identification, classification, labeling, and communication of chemical hazards to ensure that all employees are informed about the substances they may encounter. Effective hazard communication is essential for preventing accidents and illnesses in environments where chemicals are used or stored.

Importance of Hazard Communications

The primary purpose of hazard communication is to protect employee health and safety by ensuring that all workers are fully aware of the chemicals they work with, along with their potential hazards. This knowledge helps workers handle chemicals safely and respond appropriately in emergency situations, reducing the risk of exposure to harmful substances.

Key Components of Hazard Communication

1. Chemical Inventory: Organizations must maintain an up-to-date inventory of all hazardous chemicals in their workplaces. This inventory serves as the foundation for all other aspects of hazard communication.

2. Safety Data Sheets (SDS): Safety Data Sheets provide detailed information about each hazardous chemical, including its properties, health effects, safety precautions, and emergency response procedures. SDSs must be accessible to all employees at all times.

3. Labeling: All containers of hazardous chemicals must be clearly labeled with the chemical identity, hazard warnings, and the name and address of the manufacturer or other responsible party. Labels must be legible, prominently displayed, and resistant to environmental damage.

4. Employee Training and Information: Employers are required to train all workers on the hazards of the chemicals they might encounter in their work areas and on proper handling and emergency procedures before job assignment and whenever a new hazard is introduced.

Regulations and Standards

1. OSHA's Hazard Communication Standard (HCS): In the United States, the Occupational Safety and Health Administration (OSHA) regulates hazard communication under the Hazard Communication Standard (HCS), also known as the "right-to-know" law. This standard requires chemical manufacturers, distributors, and importers to provide the aforementioned safety data sheets and ensures that employers communicate these hazards to employees.

2. Globally Harmonized System (GHS): The Globally Harmonized System of Classification and Labeling of Chemicals (GHS) is an international standard that aims to standardize the classification and labeling of chemicals globally. Its adoption into national regulations helps ensure that the hazards of chemicals are communicated uniformly worldwide.

Challenges in Hazard Communication

1. Compliance Across Jurisdictions: Managing compliance with different hazard communication standards across jurisdictions can be challenging, especially for multinational corporations that must navigate varying requirements.

2. Language and Literacy Barriers: Providing training and materials in a format that is accessible to all employees, regardless of their language skills or literacy levels, is crucial but often difficult to achieve.

3. Keeping Information Up-to-Date: Chemical inventories and safety data sheets must be regularly reviewed and updated to reflect any new scientific information or changes in regulations. This requires ongoing vigilance and resource allocation.

Best Practices for Effective Hazard Communication

1. Regular Audits: Conducting regular audits of hazard communication practices ensures compliance and identifies areas for improvement.

2. Digital Management Systems: Utilizing digital systems to manage safety data sheets and chemical inventories can improve accessibility and ease of maintenance.

3. Continuous Training: Beyond initial training, continuous education on hazard communication helps keep safety a priority and ensures that all employees are aware of the latest safety practices and standards.

Conclusion

Hazard communications play a vital role in maintaining a safe working environment, especially in industries where chemical exposure is a risk. By effectively managing hazard communication, organizations not only comply with legal requirements but also foster a safety culture that prioritizes the well-being of every employee. Effective hazard communication is not just about fulfilling regulatory obligations—it is about ensuring that all employees return home safely at the end of the day.

Problems:

Problem 1: Industrial Hygiene What is the primary purpose of conducting air quality monitoring in an industrial setting?

Problem 2: Safety Equipment Which type of safety equipment would be most appropriate for protecting workers from high decibel noise in a manufacturing plant?

Problem 3: Gas Detection and Monitoring What is the main advantage of using infrared sensors over catalytic sensors for gas detection in environments with high levels of volatile organic compounds?

Problem 4: Electrical Safety What is the primary safety concern when using portable electric tools in wet conditions?

Problem 5: Confined Space Entry Why is it necessary to perform continuous atmospheric testing when workers are inside a confined space?

Problem 6: Hazard Communications What information must always be included on the label of a chemical container according to OSHA's Hazard Communication Standard?

Problem 7: Industrial Hygiene Describe a scenario where the use of personal protective equipment (PPE) is necessary even after implementing engineering controls.

Problem 8: Safety Equipment What is the role of a ground fault circuit interrupter (GFCI) in electrical safety?

Problem 9: Gas Detection and Monitoring How should a facility store and maintain portable gas detectors to ensure reliability and accuracy?

Problem 10: Confined Space Entry What is the most critical safety measure to implement before allowing workers to enter a tank that previously contained flammable liquids?

Solutions:

Solution 1: The primary purpose of air quality monitoring in an industrial setting is to identify and quantify airborne contaminants that may pose health risks to workers, ensuring that exposure levels do not exceed regulatory and health safety standards.

Solution 2: Earmuffs or earplugs are appropriate for protecting workers from high decibel noise in a manufacturing plant, as they can significantly reduce noise exposure levels and prevent hearing damage.

Solution 3: The main advantage of using infrared sensors over catalytic sensors is that infrared sensors do not require oxygen to function and are not poisoned by substances that typically deactivate catalytic sensors. This makes them more reliable in environments with high levels of volatile organic compounds.

Solution 4: The primary safety concern when using portable electric tools in wet conditions is the increased risk of electric shock. Using tools that are double-insulated or connected to a ground fault circuit interrupter (GFCI) can mitigate this risk.

Solution 5: Continuous atmospheric testing in a confined space is necessary to ensure that the environment remains safe for workers, as changes in conditions (such as oxygen levels, toxic gas concentrations, and explosive gases) can occur rapidly and without visible warning.

Solution 6: According to OSHA's Hazard Communication Standard, the label of a chemical container must include the chemical identity, appropriate hazard warnings, and the manufacturer's or distributor's name and address.

Solution 7: A scenario where the use of PPE is necessary even after implementing engineering controls could involve handling hazardous chemicals where engineering controls reduce but do not eliminate exposure. For example, when using a fume hood in a laboratory, technicians may still need to wear gloves and goggles to protect against splashes and residual vapors.

Solution 8: The role of a ground fault circuit interrupter (GFCI) is to protect users from electrical shock by quickly cutting off power if an imbalance between incoming and outgoing current is detected, which is indicative of a leakage current that could pass through a person.

Solution 9: To ensure reliability and accuracy, portable gas detectors should be stored in environments that do not expose them to extreme temperatures or contaminants. Regular calibration and maintenance according to the manufacturer's recommendations are also crucial.

Solution 10: The most critical safety measure before allowing workers to enter a tank that previously contained flammable liquids is to ensure the tank is properly ventilated and to test the atmosphere for flammable gases to confirm that it is safe to enter.

Chapter 7: Engineering Economics

Time Value of Money

The concept of the Time Value of Money (TVM) is foundational in engineering economics, finance, and investment decision-making. It is based on the principle that a dollar available today is worth more than a dollar available in the future due to its potential earning capacity. This core principle helps engineers and financial analysts assess the value of investments, compare projects, and make informed economic decisions that maximize value.

Understanding Time Value of Money

1. Present Value (PV): Present value is the current worth of a future sum of money or stream of cash flows given a specified rate of return. Future cash flows are discounted at the discount rate, and the higher the discount rate, the lower the present value of the future cash flows.

2. Future Value (FV): Future value is the value of a current asset at a specified date in the future based on an assumed rate of growth. The future value measures how much an investment made today will grow to at some future date.

3. Net Present Value (NPV): Net Present Value is a standard method for using the time value of money to appraise long-term projects. It represents the difference between the present value of cash inflows and the present value of cash outflows over a period of time.

4. Annuities and Perpetuities: An annuity is a series of equal payments at regular intervals for a specific period of time. Annuities can be valued using the present value and future value concepts, which are essential for calculating loans, mortgages, and retirement funds. A perpetuity is an annuity that lasts forever.

Applying Time Value of Money in Engineering Decisions

1. Investment Analysis: Engineers use TVM to evaluate the profitability of projects and investments. By calculating the future value of expected cash flows, they can determine if the returns meet the required financial thresholds.

2. Cost-Benefit Analysis: In cost-benefit analysis, the time value of money is used to compare the costs and benefits that occur at different times. This analysis helps in determining whether the benefits of a project outweigh its costs and by how much.

3. Loan and Mortgage Calculations: Understanding the mechanics of TVM allows engineers to calculate the payments for loans and mortgages, which are typically structured as annuities.

4. Retirement Planning: Engineers often contribute to designing pension plans and retirement funds. TVM is crucial in determining how much money needs to be saved and how these savings grow over time.

Tools and Techniques for Time Value of Money Calculations

1. Discounting and Compounding: Discounting is the process of determining the present value of an amount that is received in the future. Compounding is the process by which an investment grows when interest is earned on both the initial principal and the accumulated interest.

2. Financial Calculators and Software: Financial calculators and software programs are widely used for TVM calculations. They help perform complex calculations that involve factors like compounding periods, variable interest rates, and different cash flow scenarios.

3. Formulas: Several key formulas are used in TVM calculations, including:

- Present Value Formula: $PV = \frac{FV}{(1+r)^n}$
- Future Value Formula: $FV = PV \times (1+r)^n$
- NPV Formula: $NPV = \sum \frac{C_t}{(1+r)^t}$

Challenges with Time Value of Money

1. Estimating Future Cash Flows: Predicting future cash flows accurately is challenging due to economic fluctuations, market dynamics, and unforeseen events.

2. Determining the Appropriate Discount Rate: Selecting the right discount rate is crucial, as it significantly affects the present value calculations. This rate should reflect the risk of the investment and opportunity cost.

Conclusion

The Time Value of Money is a critical concept in engineering economics, providing a systematic approach to evaluating the economic viability of projects. It allows engineers to make informed decisions that align with financial objectives and ensure the best use of capital. Understanding and applying TVM concepts effectively can lead to more strategic and profitable project outcomes.

Cost Analysis

Cost analysis in engineering economics is a fundamental method used to evaluate the financial aspects of projects and business operations. It involves the systematic approach of identifying, recording, and analyzing costs associated with a project to determine its overall financial feasibility. Effective cost analysis aids in budgeting, financial planning, and helps in making informed strategic decisions.

Importance of Cost Analysis

The primary purpose of cost analysis is to ensure that resources are used efficiently and economically. By understanding all costs involved in a project, engineers and managers can make more accurate projections, avoid cost overruns, and improve profitability. It also allows for better control over expenditures and aids in identifying areas where cost reductions can be achieved.

Components of Cost Analysis

1. Direct Costs: These are expenses that are directly attributable to a specific project or activity. Direct costs include materials, labor, equipment, and services consumed in the production of goods or services. Accurately attributing direct costs is crucial for precise cost analysis and pricing strategies.

2. Indirect Costs: Indirect costs, or overheads, are not directly traceable to a specific project but are necessary for the operations of the company. These include administration, utilities, security, and support staff salaries. Allocation of indirect costs needs to be handled with methods that reflect their true consumption by different projects.

3. Fixed and Variable Costs:

- **Fixed Costs:** These costs do not change with the level of production or service delivery. Examples include rent, salaries, and insurance.
- **Variable Costs:** These costs vary directly with the level of production. This includes materials, direct labor, and utility costs used in manufacturing.

4. Sunk Costs: Sunk costs are expenditures that have already been incurred and cannot be recovered. These costs should not influence future decisions but are important for project evaluation and financial analysis.

5. Opportunity Costs: Opportunity cost represents the benefits an entity misses out on when choosing one alternative over another. This is crucial in project selection and capital budgeting to ensure the most lucrative opportunities are pursued.

Techniques in Cost Analysis

1. Break-even Analysis: This technique determines the point at which the costs of producing a product equal the revenue made from selling the product. It helps in understanding the minimum production and sales level necessary to cover all costs.

2. Cost-Benefit Analysis: Cost-benefit analysis compares the costs and benefits of a decision, project, or policy. It involves quantifying the costs and benefits in monetary terms to calculate the net benefit or cost associated with the options under consideration.

3. Life Cycle Cost Analysis (LCCA): LCCA is used to assess the total cost of ownership of a project. It includes initial costs, operation, maintenance, and eventual disposal costs. This is particularly important in projects where long-term costs might outweigh initial investments.

Challenges in Cost Analysis

1. Inaccurate Cost Estimation: Estimating costs accurately can be challenging due to unforeseen factors such as economic fluctuations, changes in material costs, and technical issues during execution.

2. Allocating Indirect Costs: Properly allocating indirect costs to various projects or departments can be complex but is essential for true cost visibility.

3. Time-Value of Money: Cost analyses for long-term projects need to consider the time-value of money, which can complicate the calculations but is necessary for accurate financial assessment.

Conclusion

Cost analysis is a vital component of engineering economic decision-making. It provides a detailed examination of financial expenditures related to projects and operations, facilitating better management and optimization of resources. Mastery of various cost analysis techniques enables engineers and managers to enhance project planning, execution, and ultimately lead to more successful project outcomes and profitability.

Economic Analysis Techniques

Economic analysis techniques in engineering are essential for evaluating the economic viability and potential profitability of projects. These methodologies help engineers and decision-makers compare different projects, make investment decisions, and allocate resources effectively by analyzing the economic implications of project alternatives under various constraints and scenarios.

Key Economic Analysis Techniques

1. Net Present Value (NPV): NPV is a critical method used to evaluate the profitability of an investment. It calculates the difference between the present value of cash inflows and the present value of cash outflows over a project's lifetime. A positive NPV indicates that the projected earnings generated by a project or investment—in present dollars—exceed the anticipated costs, also in present dollars.

2. Internal Rate of Return (IRR): IRR is the discount rate that makes the NPV of all cash flows from a particular project equal to zero. This rate is a commonly used indicator of a project's efficiency or quality; the higher the IRR, the more desirable the project is likely to be. IRR is particularly useful for ranking multiple prospective projects.

3. Payback Period: The payback period is the time it takes for the cash inflows from a capital investment project to equal the cash outflows. This method is easy to understand and use but ignores the time value of money, which can be a significant drawback when comparing projects with different cash flow patterns.

4. Benefit-Cost Ratio (BCR): The BCR is a ratio that helps evaluate the relationship between the relative costs and benefits of a project, expressed in monetary terms. A ratio greater than one indicates that the benefits outweigh the costs, suggesting the project is economically viable.

5. Sensitivity Analysis: Sensitivity analysis examines how different values of an independent variable affect a particular dependent variable under a given set of assumptions. This technique is used to predict the outcome of a decision if a situation turns out to be different compared to the key predictions.

6. Break-even Analysis: Break-even analysis determines when an investment will generate a positive return. It calculates the point, usually in terms of sales or units produced, at which total revenues equal total costs. This method is particularly useful for new businesses and for evaluating the profitability of a new product.

Applications of Economic Analysis Techniques

1. Project Selection: These techniques are crucial in project selection, enabling engineers and managers to quantify the economic benefits of different projects and determine the best alternatives under capital constraints.

2. Budgeting and Forecasting: Economic analysis is integral to the budgeting and financial forecasting processes, helping predict future financial needs, revenues, and expenses associated with projects.

3. Risk Management: Economic analysis techniques like sensitivity and scenario analysis help in understanding and managing the risks associated with project uncertainties.

4. Performance Evaluation: Post-implementation reviews of projects often use economic analysis to assess whether or not, and to what extent, a project has achieved its intended economic goals.

Challenges in Economic Analysis

1. Data Quality and Availability: Accurate economic analysis depends heavily on the quality and availability of data. Inaccurate or incomplete data can lead to faulty conclusions.

2. Handling Uncertainty: Projects often involve uncertainties related to market conditions, technological changes, and regulatory environments. Accounting for these uncertainties in economic evaluations is challenging but essential.

3. Complexity of Analysis: Some economic analysis techniques can become complex, especially when dealing with large projects that have multiple alternatives and variable factors.

Conclusion

Economic analysis techniques are indispensable tools in engineering that provide a robust framework for making informed decisions. They help in evaluating the economic feasibility of projects, optimizing resource allocation, and enhancing the overall strategic decision-making process. Mastery of these techniques allows engineers to add significant value to their projects, ensuring that investments are not only feasible but also optimal under various economic conditions.

Dealing with Uncertainty in Economic Analysis

Uncertainty is an inherent aspect of engineering and economic analysis, stemming from unpredictable variables such as market fluctuations, technological changes, regulatory shifts, and environmental conditions. Effective management of uncertainty is crucial in ensuring that economic analyses remain robust and that decision-making processes lead to sustainable and profitable outcomes.

Understanding Uncertainty in Economic Analysis

Uncertainty in economic analysis can be categorized into several types:

1. Project-Specific Uncertainty: This relates to unknowns directly connected to a project, such as construction delays, cost overruns, and technical failures.

2. Economic Uncertainty: Includes factors such as inflation rates, interest rates, and economic growth that can impact the financial viability of a project.

3. Political and Regulatory Uncertainty: Changes in laws, regulations, or government policies can alter the economic landscape dramatically and unpredictably.

4. Market and Demand Uncertainty: Fluctuations in market demand, prices, and competition can affect the projected returns from a project.

Techniques for Managing Uncertainty

Effective strategies and tools are necessary to handle uncertainty in economic analysis. These include:

1. Sensitivity Analysis: This technique involves changing one variable at a time to see how it affects the outcome of the analysis. It helps identify which variables have the most impact on the project's outcome and which are less influential.

2. Scenario Analysis: Unlike sensitivity analysis, scenario analysis examines the changes in multiple variables simultaneously to assess potential outcomes under different scenarios. This approach helps in understanding the best and worst cases and everything in between.

3. Monte Carlo Simulations: This method uses probability distributions and random sampling to simulate a range of possible outcomes in a complex project. It provides a probability distribution of the possible outcomes rather than a single static result.

4. Real Options Analysis: Real options analysis provides a methodological approach for making decisions in a multi-stage project with uncertainty. It treats investment decisions as "options" that can be altered in the future as uncertainty unfolds.

5. Risk Management Planning: Involves identifying potential risks, assessing their likelihood and potential impacts, and preparing strategies to mitigate these risks. Effective risk management can reduce both the likelihood and impact of adverse conditions.

Application of Uncertainty Analysis

1. Project Evaluation and Selection: Handling uncertainty is crucial in project evaluation and selection, ensuring that decisions are made based on comprehensive risk-adjusted analyses rather than optimistic forecasts.

2. Financial Planning and Budgeting: Financial plans and budgets that consider uncertainty can accommodate unexpected changes, ensuring that a project remains viable under various conditions.

3. Strategic Planning: Incorporating uncertainty into strategic planning helps businesses prepare for future challenges and leverage opportunities as they arise.

Challenges in Managing Uncertainty

1. Quantifying Uncertainty: One of the main challenges is quantifying uncertainty accurately. Many uncertainties are qualitative and cannot easily be expressed in numerical terms.

2. Dynamic Variables: The variables associated with uncertainty can change rapidly, requiring continuous monitoring and updating of economic analyses to remain relevant.

3. Decision-Maker Bias: Cognitive biases can affect how uncertainty is perceived and managed. Overconfidence, for instance, can lead to underestimating risks.

Conclusion

Dealing with uncertainty in economic analysis requires a systematic approach to identify, assess, and mitigate risks. By employing techniques such as sensitivity and scenario analyses, Monte Carlo simulations, and real options analysis, engineers and economists can better manage the inherent uncertainties of projects. This leads to more informed and resilient decision-making, ensuring that projects are not only feasible but also adaptable to changing conditions. Effective uncertainty management is not about eliminating risk but about understanding it and preparing to handle its impacts, thereby safeguarding project investments and enhancing their likelihood of success.

Project Selection Methods

Project selection methods are critical tools in engineering and business that guide decision-makers in choosing between multiple project alternatives based on their economic viability, strategic alignment, and potential benefits. Effective project selection ensures optimal allocation of resources, maximizes returns, and aligns with the organization's long-term goals.

Importance of Project Selection

The right project selection can lead to substantial financial and strategic benefits for an organization. Conversely, selecting a suboptimal project can result in wasted resources, missed opportunities, and even financial losses. The method used for project selection can greatly influence the outcome, making it crucial for organizations to employ robust, comprehensive techniques that consider various factors beyond mere financial returns.

Common Project Selection Methods

1. Net Present Value (NPV): NPV is a fundamental financial analysis tool used to assess the profitability of a project by discounting future cash flows to their present value. A project with a positive NPV is typically considered financially viable because it is expected to generate net returns over its cost.

2. Internal Rate of Return (IRR): IRR is the discount rate at which the NPV of all the cash flows from a particular project equals zero. Projects with an IRR that exceeds the cost of capital are generally considered acceptable as they promise returns greater than the minimum rate required by investors.

3. Payback Period: The payback period is the time it takes for the cash inflows from a capital investment project to repay the initial investment cost. Shorter payback periods are preferred as they imply quicker recovery of invested funds and reduced exposure to risk.

4. Profitability Index (PI): Also known as the benefit-cost ratio, the PI is the ratio of the present value of future expected cash flows divided by the initial investment. A PI greater than 1.0 indicates that the NPV is positive, suggesting the project is economically justified.

5. Real Options Analysis (ROA): ROA considers the flexibility of managing projects in a dynamic environment where future conditions are uncertain. It values the choices embedded in investment opportunities as real options, similar to financial options.

6. Scoring Models: Scoring models are used for project selection by evaluating multiple criteria, including but not limited to economic factors. Projects are scored based on their performance against these criteria, and weights are assigned to reflect the relative importance of each factor.

7. Decision Trees: Decision trees help in making sequential decisions under uncertainty. They provide a graphical representation of alternatives and their possible outcomes, including risks, costs, and benefits, helping to choose the path that maximizes potential returns.

Applications of Project Selection Methods

1. Capital Budgeting: These methods are extensively used in capital budgeting to determine which projects to invest in, ensuring that capital expenditures are made in projects that yield the best returns over their useful life.

2. Strategic Business Decisions: Beyond financial implications, project selection methods are crucial for strategic decision-making, helping align projects with business strategies and market conditions.

3. Risk Management: Incorporating risk assessments into project selection helps identify projects that offer sustainable returns while managing potential risks effectively.

Challenges in Project Selection

1. Complexity of Analysis: Many project selection methods require complex financial modeling and assumptions, which can introduce significant uncertainty into the decision-making process.

2. Subjectivity in Non-Financial Factors: Incorporating non-financial factors such as environmental impact, social responsibility, or employee satisfaction introduces subjectivity, making the decision process more complex.

3. Dynamic Market Conditions: Rapid changes in market or technological conditions can quickly render a project selection decision obsolete, requiring continuous review and adaptability.

Conclusion

Project selection methods are essential in guiding organizations through the process of evaluating and choosing projects based on a comprehensive assessment of financial metrics, strategic fit, and risk considerations. Mastery of these techniques enables decision-makers to undertake projects that not only promise the best financial returns but also align with broader organizational objectives and adapt to changing environmental and market conditions.

Problems:

Problem 1: Time Value of Money Calculate the future value of $10,000 invested today at an annual interest rate of 5% for 5 years.

Problem 2: Cost Analysis Determine the break-even point in units for a product with a selling price of $20 per unit, variable costs of $12 per unit, and fixed costs of $8,000.

Problem 3: Economic Analysis Techniques What is the net present value (NPV) of a project that requires an initial investment of $50,000 and provides annual cash flows of $15,000 for 5 years, if the discount rate is 10%?

Problem 4: Dealing with Uncertainty in Economic Analysis Describe one method to handle risk when evaluating a project with uncertain future cash flows.

Problem 5: Project Selection Methods If a project has cash inflows of $20,000 per year for three years and an initial cost of $50,000, calculate the internal rate of return (IRR).

Problem 6: Time Value of Money What is the present value of a $5,000 payment to be received in 4 years if the discount rate is 6% per annum?

Problem 7: Cost Analysis If a company reduces its variable costs by 10% while maintaining the same selling price, how does this affect the break-even volume?

Problem 8: Economic Analysis Techniques Explain the difference between the internal rate of return (IRR) and the return on investment (ROI).

Problem 9: Dealing with Uncertainty in Economic Analysis How can Monte Carlo simulations be used in economic analysis?

Problem 10: Project Selection Methods Compare and contrast the use of NPV and Payback Period as methods for project selection.

Solutions:

Solution 1:
$$FV = PV \times (1+r)^n = \$10,000 \times (1+0.05)^5 = \$10,000 \times 1.2763 = \$12,763$$

Solution 2:
$$Break-even\ point = \frac{Fixed\ Costs}{Selling\ Price - Variable\ Costs} = \frac{\$8,000}{\$20 - \$12} = \frac{\$8,000}{\$8} = 1,000\ units$$

Solution 3:
$$NPV = -\$50,000 + \frac{\$15,000}{1.1} + \frac{\$15,000}{1.1^2} + \frac{\$15,000}{1.1^3} + \frac{\$15,000}{1.1^4} + \frac{\$15,000}{1.1^5} = -\$50,000 + \$13,636 + \$12,396 + \$11,269 + \$10,245 + \$9,314 = \$6,860$$

Solution 4:
Using sensitivity analysis to vary each uncertain cash flow input and observe the impact on the project's NPV or IRR can help handle risk and identify critical variables.

Solution 5:
$$0 = -\$50,000 + \frac{\$20,000}{1+r} + \frac{\$20,000}{(1+r)^2} + \frac{\$20,000}{(1+r)^3}$$
This equation needs to be solved iteratively or using financial software to find r, which is the IRR.

Solution 6:
$$PV = \frac{FV}{(1+r)^n} = \frac{\$5,000}{(1+0.06)^4} = \frac{\$5,000}{1.2625} = \$3,959$$

Solution 7:
Reducing variable costs decreases the contribution margin per unit, leading to a lower break-even volume. Specifically, it would decrease by 10% under the same calculation as before, improving profitability.

Solution 8:
IRR is the rate that makes the NPV of cash flows equal to zero and is a profitability measure from an investment perspective. ROI measures the efficiency of an investment and is calculated as the ratio of the net gain to the cost of the investment.

Solution 9:
Monte Carlo simulations use random sampling and statistical modeling to estimate mathematical functions and mimic the operation of complex systems to predict project risks and outcomes.

Solution 10:
NPV provides a dollar value that represents the net value added by the project and considers the time value of money, making it more comprehensive for long-term projects. The Payback Period identifies how quickly an investment can be recovered, which is simpler but ignores the benefits beyond the payback point and the time value of money.

Chapter 8: Statics

Vector Analysis

Vector analysis is a fundamental component of statics, the branch of mechanics that deals with the analysis of forces on physical bodies in a state where they remain at rest or move at a constant velocity. Vectors are mathematical representations of quantities possessing both magnitude and direction, making them crucial for describing forces, velocities, and other directional quantities in engineering applications.

Fundamentals of Vectors

1. Definition and Representation: A vector is represented graphically by an arrow. The length of the arrow indicates the vector's magnitude, while its orientation in space shows the direction. In statics, vectors are used to represent physical quantities such as displacement, force, and momentum.

2. Vector Operations:

- **Addition:** Vectors are added using the triangle or parallelogram law, where the resultant vector is derived by placing vectors tip to tail or by connecting the diagonals of a parallelogram formed by the vectors.

- **Subtraction:** Vector subtraction can be visualized as the addition of a negative vector. The difference between two vectors is a vector that, when added to the second vector, results in the first vector.

- **Scalar Multiplication:** Multiplying a vector by a scalar changes the magnitude of the vector without altering its direction.

3. Components of Vectors: Vectors can be broken down into components, which are projections along the axes of a coordinate system. This decomposition simplifies the analysis of vectors, especially when dealing with multiple vector quantities in physics and engineering.

Vector Analysis in Statics

1. Force Vectors: In statics, forces are represented as vectors because they have both magnitude and direction. Understanding how forces interact through vector addition is fundamental to solving static equilibrium problems.

2. Equilibrium Conditions: For a system to be in static equilibrium, the sum of all force vectors acting on the system must be zero. This condition is expressed as the vector sum of forces equaling zero, known as the first condition of equilibrium. The second condition of equilibrium states that the sum of all moments about any point must also be zero.

3. Torque Vectors: Torque, a measure of the force causing an object to rotate, is a vector quantity. The direction of the torque vector depends on the direction of the force and the point about which the force is applied.

Applications of Vector Analysis in Engineering

1. Structural Analysis: Engineers use vector analysis to determine the forces acting on structural components such as beams, trusses, and frames, ensuring they are designed to withstand expected loads.

2. Mechanical Systems: Vector methods are crucial in the design and analysis of mechanical systems, where components must be in mechanical equilibrium.

3. Robotics and Automation: In robotics, vector analysis is used to control the position and orientation of robots. Vectors describe the movement of robotic arms and the forces they apply while interacting with objects.

Challenges in Vector Analysis

1. Complexity in Three-dimensional Space: While vector operations in two dimensions are relatively straightforward, extending these operations to three dimensions can significantly complicate analysis, particularly in determining the direction and magnitude of resultant vectors.

2. Accuracy in Measurements: The precision of vector quantities depends heavily on the accuracy of the initial measurements of magnitude and direction, which can be challenging in practical engineering applications.

Conclusion

Vector analysis is a powerful tool in statics, providing a clear mathematical framework for dealing with forces and other physical quantities in engineering. By mastering vector operations and understanding their applications in static equilibrium and beyond, engineers can design safer and more efficient structures and mechanical systems. This deep understanding of vectors ensures that engineers can solve complex problems in statics with confidence and precision.

Force Systems

In the realm of statics, understanding force systems is crucial for analyzing the effects of forces on physical structures and mechanical systems. Force systems refer to a collection of forces acting on a body, which can influence the body's state of rest or uniform motion. Effective analysis of these systems enables engineers to design structures and mechanisms that can withstand applied loads without failure.

Types of Force Systems

1. Coplanar Force Systems: Forces that lie within a single plane are referred to as coplanar forces. They are commonly encountered in structural engineering and simple machinery and can be further categorized into concurrent, parallel, and general systems based on the lines of action of the forces.

- **Concurrent:** All force lines of action intersect at a common point.
- **Parallel:** All forces are parallel to each other.
- **General:** Forces are neither concurrent nor parallel but act within the same plane.

2. Non-Coplanar Force Systems: Non-coplanar forces do not lie within a single plane and are essential in analyzing spatial structures like trusses used in bridges and aerial structures. These can also be concurrent or non-concurrent.

3. Collinear Force Systems: In collinear force systems, all the forces are along the same line of action, often seen in cable systems or in objects being pulled or pushed in a straight line.

Analysis of Force Systems

1. Resultant Forces: The resultant of a force system is a single force or moment that represents the effect of all the individual forces acting together. Calculating the resultant force involves vector addition where forces are added head-to-tail or using algebraic methods for components.

2. Equilibrium Equations: For a body to be in static equilibrium under the action of a force system, the sum of all forces and the sum of all moments about any point must be zero. These conditions are expressed as:

- $\Sigma F = 0$ (Sum of horizontal forces = 0; Sum of vertical forces = 0)
- $\Sigma M = 0$ (Sum of moments about any point = 0)

3. Free-Body Diagrams (FBDs): Free-body diagrams are crucial in the analysis of force systems, as they help isolate the body or component and show all the forces acting upon it, including applied forces, frictional forces, and support reactions.

Applications of Force Systems in Engineering

1. Structural Engineering: Force systems analysis enables structural engineers to design buildings, bridges, and other structures that can safely withstand various loads such as weight, wind, and seismic activities.

2. Mechanical Engineering: In mechanical systems, understanding force systems helps in designing components that perform desired motions without exceeding the strength limits of the material.

3. Aerospace Engineering: Analysis of force systems is critical in determining how forces and moments influence the flight performance and stability of aircraft.

Challenges in Force Systems Analysis

1. Complexity of Real-World Applications: Real-world applications often involve complex, three-dimensional force systems that require sophisticated calculation methods and assumptions to simplify the analysis.

2. Accuracy and Precision: Determining the accurate magnitude, direction, and point of application of forces is critical and can be challenging, especially in dynamic or fluid environments.

3. Material Behavior Under Load: Understanding how materials deform or fail under different types of force systems is crucial and requires a thorough knowledge of material mechanics and behavior.

Conclusion

Force systems are foundational elements in statics, playing a critical role across various engineering disciplines. Mastery of force system analysis is not only fundamental to ensuring the structural integrity and functionality of engineering designs but also essential in optimizing these designs for both efficiency and safety. The ability to accurately analyze and apply these concepts in real-world scenarios marks the difference between adequate and exceptional engineering solutions.

Equilibrium of Rigid Bodies

In the field of statics, the concept of equilibrium is fundamental when analyzing structures or components that must remain stationary or at constant velocity under the action of forces. Equilibrium of rigid bodies occurs when the sum of all forces and the sum of all moments acting on the body are zero, ensuring the body remains in a stable state without translational or rotational motion.

Principles of Equilibrium

1. Conditions for Equilibrium: For a rigid body to be in equilibrium, it must satisfy two primary conditions:

- **First Condition (Translational Equilibrium):** The vector sum of all forces acting on the body must be zero ($\Sigma F = 0$). This condition ensures there is no net force acting on the body, preventing linear acceleration.

- **Second Condition (Rotational Equilibrium):** The sum of all moments about any point must also be zero ($\Sigma M = 0$). This condition ensures that there is no net torque, preventing angular acceleration.

These conditions are applied in both two-dimensional and three-dimensional force systems.

2. Static Equilibrium Analysis: Static equilibrium analysis involves breaking down complex force systems into manageable components using free-body diagrams, where all external forces and moments are represented. This analysis is critical in ensuring the stability of structures and mechanical systems.

Applications in Engineering

1. Structural Engineering: Engineers use equilibrium principles to design buildings, bridges, and other structures that can withstand various loads without moving or collapsing. Ensuring that all structural components are in equilibrium under load is vital for safety and durability.

2. Mechanical Systems: In machinery and mechanical systems, ensuring the equilibrium of components like gears, levers, and beams is crucial to maintaining functional integrity and operational efficiency.

3. Robotics and Automation: In robotics, equilibrium analysis helps in designing robotic arms and other components that must perform precise movements without unwanted deviations caused by unbalanced forces or moments.

Techniques for Analyzing Equilibrium

1. Free-Body Diagrams (FBDs): Creating accurate free-body diagrams is essential for analyzing the equilibrium of rigid bodies. An FBD isolates the body from its surroundings and represents all external forces, including applied forces, gravitational forces, normal forces, frictional forces, and support reactions.

2. Equations of Equilibrium: For two-dimensional problems, the equations of equilibrium typically involve setting the sum of horizontal forces, the sum of vertical forces, and the sum of moments about a point to zero. In three dimensions, these expand to include sums in the x, y, and z directions and about multiple axes.

3. Method of Joints and Method of Sections: In truss analysis, these methods are used to solve for unknown forces in truss members, applying the conditions of equilibrium to each joint or section cut.

Challenges in Equilibrium Analysis

1. Complex Loads and Support Conditions: Analyzing bodies with complex loading or support conditions, such as variable loads or multiple support points, requires careful consideration and often advanced mathematical and computational techniques.

2. Determination of Reaction Forces: Identifying and calculating reaction forces at supports or connections can be challenging, especially when dealing with non-conventional support configurations.

3. Dynamic Stability: While static equilibrium ensures stability under static loads, dynamic stability under variable loads or during motion can complicate analysis, requiring more sophisticated modeling and simulation.

Conclusion

Understanding and applying the principles of equilibrium of rigid bodies are crucial in various branches of engineering. This knowledge ensures that structures and mechanical systems are designed to remain stable under expected loads, providing safety and functionality in everyday applications. Mastery of equilibrium concepts allows engineers to innovate and create more complex and efficient designs that push the boundaries of what is mechanically possible.

Internal Forces

In the study of statics, internal forces are the forces that act within a structure or between the elements of a mechanical system. Understanding these forces is crucial for analyzing how external loads are transmitted and distributed through a structure, which is essential for ensuring structural integrity and safety.

Fundamentals of Internal Forces

1. Definition and Importance: Internal forces are reactions to external forces, ensuring that a body remains in equilibrium. They are not directly observable but can be calculated by analyzing the sections of a structure under a given load. These forces include tension, compression, shear, bending, and torsion.

2. Types of Internal Forces:

- **Tension:** A force that pulls or stretches material along the axis of the member.
- **Compression:** A force that compresses or shortens the material.
- **Shear:** Forces that cause parts of a material to slide past each other in opposite directions.
- **Bending:** Moments that induce bending of a member about its axis.
- **Torsion:** A twisting force that results in shear stresses perpendicular to the axis of twist.

Analyzing Internal Forces

1. Free Body Diagrams (FBDs): FBDs are used to isolate a member and represent all external forces, moments, and reactions acting on it, providing a clear method to begin calculating internal forces.

2. Cut Method: To find internal forces, engineers often make an imaginary 'cut' through the structure and analyze the forces acting across the cut surface. This method reveals the internal force distribution required to keep the structure in equilibrium.

3. Equations of Equilibrium: These equations (ΣF = 0 and ΣM = 0) are applied to the free-body diagram of the cut section to solve for unknown internal forces and moments.

Applications of Internal Forces Analysis

1. Beam Bending: In civil engineering, beams subject to various loads must be analyzed to determine internal bending moments and shear forces. This analysis is critical for determining the size and material specifications needed to ensure safety and structural integrity.

2. Trusses: Truss structures, commonly used in bridges and roofs, rely on a precise understanding of internal force distribution in each member, typically assumed to be axial forces (tension or compression).

3. Mechanical Systems: In mechanical engineering, components such as shafts, couplings, and gears are designed considering internal torsion and shear forces to prevent failure during operation.

Challenges in Internal Forces Analysis

1. Complexity of Real Structures: Real-life structures can have complex loadings and constraints, making the calculation of internal forces challenging. The use of advanced computational methods and finite element analysis (FEA) software has become necessary for accurate predictions.

2. Material Properties: The behavior of internal forces depends significantly on the material properties, such as yield strength, ductility, and modulus of elasticity. Inaccurate material data can lead to erroneous force analysis.

3. Dynamic Loads: Analyzing internal forces under dynamic conditions, such as in vehicles or during seismic events, adds complexity because the forces change over time, requiring more sophisticated dynamic analysis methods.

Conclusion

Internal forces play a crucial role in the field of engineering, particularly in statics and structural analysis. A thorough understanding of how these forces work helps engineers design safer and more efficient structures and mechanical components. The ability to accurately calculate and interpret internal forces is fundamental for predicting how structures will behave under load, ensuring they meet safety standards and perform as intended throughout their service life. This knowledge not only supports the physical implementation of engineering projects but also underscores the analytical and problem-solving skills that are essential for any engineer working in the field of statics.

Area Properties

In the study of statics and structural mechanics, understanding area properties, also known as sectional properties, is crucial for analyzing how materials behave under various loading conditions. Area properties influence the stress distribution within a material, its resistance to bending, torsion, and compression, as well as its overall stability and strength.

Key Area Properties

1. Centroid: The centroid, or geometric center, of an area is a critical point that represents the average position of all the points in the shape. It is essential in determining the distribution of stress and strain within a body when it is subjected to loads.

2. Moment of Inertia (Second Moment of Area): Moment of inertia is a geometric property that reflects how an object's cross-sectional area is distributed about an axis. It is fundamental in predicting the resistance of a beam to bending and buckling under a load. Higher moments of inertia indicate greater resistance to bending and deflection.

3. Area Moment of Inertia:

- **Axial Moment of Inertia (I_x and I_y):** Reflects bending about the x or y-axis, crucial for beams in bending.
- **Polar Moment of Inertia (J):** Important for torsional analysis, indicating how a structural element will behave under twisting loads.

4. Section Modulus: The section modulus is a direct measure of the strength of a beam. It combines the beam's shape and dimensions into a single number that describes how well a beam can resist bending. It is defined as the moment of inertia divided by the distance from the centroid to the furthest point of the section.

5. Radius of Gyration: Radius of gyration is a measure that describes the distribution of an area's cross-sectional area about a centroidal axis, indicating how far from the centroid the area's mass is concentrated. It is used to assess column stability and buckling resistance.

Calculating Area Properties

1. Integration Techniques: For irregular shapes, area properties are often calculated using integral calculus. The centroid is determined by dividing the integral of a geometric property by the total area, while moments of inertia are calculated from the integral of squared distances from the axis.

2. Composite Sections: For structures made of multiple simple shapes, properties like centroids and moments of inertia are found by summing the properties of each section, considering their relative positions and orientations.

3. Tabulated Data: For standard shapes like rectangles, circles, and I-beams, area properties are often available in engineering handbooks and databases, allowing for straightforward application in design without the need for manual calculations.

Applications of Area Properties in Engineering

1. Structural Design: Engineers use area properties to design beams, columns, and other structural elements to ensure they can safely carry anticipated loads without excessive deformation or failure.

2. Mechanical Systems: In mechanical engineering, area properties are used to design components such as shafts, levers, and frames to withstand operational loads and stresses.

3. Aerospace and Automotive: Area properties are crucial in the design of lightweight yet sturdy components that can endure various operational stresses while minimizing weight.

Challenges in Analyzing Area Properties

1. Complexity of Irregular Shapes: Calculating area properties for irregularly shaped sections can be mathematically intensive and prone to error, especially without the use of computational tools.

2. Material Heterogeneity: Variations in material properties across a section can complicate the calculation and application of area properties, affecting the accuracy of stress and deformation predictions.

3. Scale Effects: In large structures, such as bridges or skyscrapers, scale effects can influence the behavior of materials, and the classical theories based on area properties may need adjustments or corrections.

Conclusion

Area properties are a fundamental aspect of engineering analysis, providing essential insights into how materials and structures behave under various loads. Mastery of these properties enables engineers to design more efficient, safe, and reliable structures and mechanical components, ensuring they perform adequately throughout their operational life while meeting all required safety and performance standards.

Static Friction

Static friction is a force that resists the initial movement of two surfaces that are in contact but not moving relative to each other. It plays a crucial role in everyday life and engineering applications, providing the necessary resistance that prevents objects from sliding. Understanding static friction is essential for designing safe and efficient machines, vehicles, structures, and other systems where contact interaction is involved.

Fundamentals of Static Friction

1. Definition and Characteristics: Static friction is the frictional force that must be overcome to start moving an object at rest. It acts in the opposite direction to the applied force and is equal in magnitude to the applied force up to a certain limit, beyond which motion begins. The maximum static friction force before movement occurs is often greater than the kinetic friction that occurs once motion has started.

2. Coefficient of Static Friction (μ_s): The coefficient of static friction is a dimensionless number that describes the ratio of the maximum static friction force to the normal force exerted between the two surfaces. It varies depending on the materials making up the contact surfaces and their surface treatments or conditions.

Calculation of Static Friction

1. Formula: The maximum force of static friction (F_friction) can be calculated using the formula:

$$F_{friction} = \mu_s \times F_{normal}$$

where μ_s is the coefficient of static friction and F_{normal} is the normal force perpendicular to the surfaces in contact.

2. Factors Influencing Static Friction:

- **Surface Material:** Different materials have varying roughness and adhesive properties, affecting friction levels.
- **Surface Condition:** Smooth, lubricated, or polished surfaces have lower coefficients of static friction compared to rough or untreated surfaces.
- **Normal Force:** Increasing the weight of an object increases the normal force, which in turn increases the static friction force proportionally.

Applications of Static Friction in Engineering

1. Vehicle Dynamics: Static friction between tires and the road surface determines the maximum acceleration and deceleration a vehicle can achieve without skidding, crucial for safe driving dynamics and vehicle design.

2. Machinery: In machinery, static friction is used to prevent slippage between components such as gears, belts, and clutches, ensuring efficient power transmission and operation.

3. Civil Engineering: Static friction principles are used in designing foundations that must resist sliding due to lateral loads such as wind or seismic activity.

4. Consumer Products: From the grip of shoes on various surfaces to the stacking of objects without slipping, static friction is a key consideration in product design for safety and usability.

Challenges in Managing Static Friction

1. Predicting Friction Coefficients: Due to the variability in surface conditions and material properties, accurately predicting the coefficient of static friction can be challenging and often requires empirical testing.

2. Environment Effects: Environmental factors such as temperature, humidity, and contaminants can significantly affect static friction, complicating the design processes for outdoor or variable environments.

3. Wear and Tear: Repeated use can alter surface characteristics, leading to changes in friction levels over the life of a component or system.

Conclusion

Static friction is a fundamental concept in statics and dynamics, integral to the design and function of countless mechanical systems and structures. Engineers must accurately understand and predict static friction to ensure safety, efficiency, and effectiveness in their designs. Despite its challenges, advancements in material science and testing technologies continue to enhance our understanding and management of static friction in engineering applications.

Free-Body Diagrams

Free-body diagrams (FBDs) are a fundamental tool in the field of engineering mechanics, particularly within the study of statics. These diagrams are essential for visualizing the forces and moments acting on a single body, isolated from its surroundings, to analyze the interactions due to these forces. Understanding how to correctly draw and interpret FBDs is crucial for solving problems related to equilibrium and dynamics in engineering systems.

Purpose of Free-Body Diagrams

The primary purpose of an FBD is to simplify complex physical situations, allowing engineers and students to focus on the analysis of forces without distraction from other elements of the structure or mechanism. FBDs help identify all the forces acting on an object, facilitating the application of Newton's laws of motion to solve for unknowns.

Components of a Free-Body Diagram

1. Body or Structure:

- The object being analyzed is represented, typically simplified to a dot or a basic shape, depending on the complexity needed in the analysis.

2. Forces:

- All forces acting on the object are represented as vectors, which include gravitational forces, applied forces, normal forces, and frictional forces. Each vector is labeled clearly to indicate its magnitude (if known) and direction.

3. Moments and Couples:

- Any moments or torques acting on the object are also represented. These might be due to forces not acting at the object's center of gravity or due to couples (pairs of equal and opposite forces whose lines of action do not coincide).

4. Support Reactions:

- For objects in contact with other bodies (like beams or frames), reactions at the supports or joints are included. These reactions depend on the type of support (fixed, pinned, roller) and must be correctly represented to ensure accurate analysis.

5. Coordinate System:

- An FBD includes a coordinate system that helps in resolving the forces into their components, simplifying calculations especially when dealing with inclined planes or non-vertical/horizontal forces.

Steps to Construct Free-Body Diagrams

1. Isolate the Object:

- Remove the object from its surroundings mentally or graphically, focusing only on the body under consideration.

2. Sketch the Outline:

- Draw a simple outline of the object. For complex objects, it might be helpful to simplify the shape to basic geometrical forms.

3. Apply Forces and Moments:

- Accurately draw all forces and label each with its type and magnitude (if known). Use arrows to show direction, ensuring the length of each arrow accurately reflects the force's relative magnitude.

4. Indicate Support Reactions:

- Clearly show and label all reactions at supports or connections. The type of reaction will depend on the nature of the support.

5. Define Sign Conventions and Coordinates:

- Establish a coordinate system and sign conventions for the forces and moments to maintain consistency in your calculations.

Applications of Free-Body Diagrams in Engineering

1. Structural Engineering:

- Analyze forces in beams, trusses, and frames to determine the stresses and reactions at supports.

2. Mechanical Engineering:

- Design mechanical systems such as gears and levers, ensuring all forces are balanced to prevent unwanted movement or failure.

3. Aerospace Engineering:

- Calculate lift, drag, and other aerodynamic forces acting on aircraft components.

Challenges in Using Free-Body Diagrams

1. Complexity of Systems:

- Real-world structures can be complex, and simplifying them into FBDs while retaining all necessary force information can be challenging.

2. Determination of Unknown Forces:

- Often, many forces and reactions are not directly measurable and must be calculated using equilibrium equations, requiring accurate initial assumptions and calculations.

3. Over-Simplification:

- Simplifying complex systems into basic diagrams can sometimes lead to overlooking critical forces or interactions, potentially leading to errors in analysis.

Conclusion

Free-body diagrams are an indispensable tool in the arsenal of any engineer. Mastery of FBDs enables clearer understanding and more accurate analysis of physical systems, leading to better-designed, safer, and more efficient engineering solutions. As engineers advance in their careers, the ability to quickly and accurately sketch and analyze FBDs becomes a valuable skill, facilitating effective problem-solving and innovation in various engineering fields.

Weight and Mass Computations

In the realm of engineering statics, understanding the distinctions and relationships between weight and mass is crucial for accurately analyzing forces and designing structures and mechanical systems. Weight is the force exerted by gravity on an object's mass, and both play fundamental roles in the stability and functionality of engineering projects.

Fundamentals of Mass

1. Definition of Mass: Mass is a measure of the amount of matter in an object, which remains constant irrespective of the object's location in the universe. It is a scalar quantity and is fundamental in the formulation of Newton's laws of motion.

2. Units of Mass: The standard unit of mass in the International System of Units (SI) is the kilogram (kg). In the engineering field, particularly in countries using the Imperial system, mass may also be expressed in slugs.

Fundamentals of Weight

1. Definition of Weight: Weight is a vector quantity that measures the gravitational force exerted on an object's mass. Unlike mass, weight varies with the acceleration due to gravity, which can differ depending on the location (e.g., varying on Earth's surface, the moon, etc.).

2. Units of Weight: In the SI system, weight is measured in newtons (N), while in the Imperial system, pounds (lbs) are used. One newton is defined as the force required to accelerate one kilogram of mass at a rate of one meter per second squared.

Weight and Mass Computations

1. Calculating Mass: Mass is typically given or can be derived from weight if the acceleration due to gravity is known, using the formula:

$$m = \frac{W}{g}$$

where mmm is the mass, W is the weight, and g is the acceleration due to gravity.

2. Calculating Weight: Weight can be calculated if the mass of an object and the acceleration due to gravity are known:

$$W = m \times g$$

where W is the weight, mmm is the mass, and g is the local acceleration due to gravity, approximately 9.81 m/s² on Earth's surface.

Importance in Engineering Applications

1. Structural Engineering: Weight calculations are essential in structural engineering to ensure structures can support the expected loads, including the self-weight of the structure and any live loads it must bear.

2. Mechanical Engineering: In mechanical engineering, understanding the weight and mass of components is crucial for dynamic analysis, designing machinery and vehicles that perform optimally under various operational conditions.

3. Aerospace Engineering: For aerospace applications, precise weight and mass computations are vital for ensuring aircraft and spacecraft perform as expected, considering the different gravitational forces encountered.

Challenges in Weight and Mass Computations

1. Accuracy of Data: Obtaining accurate measurements of mass and accounting for variations in local gravity are crucial for precise weight calculations. Errors in these measurements can significantly affect engineering analyses and designs.

2. Variable Gravity Conditions: For projects that involve different gravitational environments (such as those in aerospace engineering), engineers must adjust their calculations to account for these differences, adding complexity to the design and analysis process.

3. Integration into Design: Integrating weight and mass considerations effectively into engineering designs requires careful planning and optimization to balance performance, safety, and cost.

Conclusion

Weight and mass computations form the backbone of many engineering processes, from the design and analysis of simple machines to complex structures and vehicles. A deep understanding of how to calculate and apply these concepts is essential for engineers across all disciplines to ensure the safety, functionality, and efficiency of their projects. Mastery of these calculations not only helps in designing better systems but also in troubleshooting and optimizing existing systems to handle various operational stresses and environmental conditions.

Problems:

Problem 1: Vector Analysis Calculate the resultant vector of two forces, one of 50 N directed north and another of 30 N directed east.

Problem 2: Force Systems Determine the equilibrium force required to balance a horizontal force system where two forces of 10 N and 15 N are acting to the right, and a third force of 5 N is acting to the left.

Problem 3: Equilibrium of Rigid Bodies A beam is supported at two ends and subjected to a downward force of 500 N at its center. Calculate the reactions at the supports if the beam is in static equilibrium.

Problem 4: Internal Forces Find the internal normal force at a point in a rod subjected to a tensile load of 1000 N.

Problem 5: Area Properties Calculate the centroid of a right triangle with a base of 3 m and a height of 4 m.

Problem 6: Static Friction If the coefficient of static friction between a box and the floor is 0.4, and the normal force is 200 N, what is the maximum static friction force that can act on the box?

Problem 7: Free-Body Diagrams Draw the free-body diagram of a block resting on a slope that makes a 30-degree angle with the horizontal, subjected to a gravitational force downward.

Problem 8: Weight and Mass Computations Calculate the weight of an object with a mass of 10 kg on Earth (g = 9.81 m/s²).

Problem 9: Equilibrium of Rigid Bodies For a ladder leaning against a smooth wall with no friction, determine the normal force exerted by the ground if the ladder has a weight of 200 N and forms a 45-degree angle with the ground.

Problem 10: Area Properties Determine the moment of inertia of a rectangle about its base, with a height of 2 m and a base of 3 m.

Solutions:

Solution 1: Resultant vector = $\sqrt{(50^2 + 30^2)}$ = $\sqrt{(2500 + 900)}$ = $\sqrt{3400}$ = 58.31 N.

Solution 2: Equilibrium force = 10 N + 15 N - 5 N = 20 N to the right.

Solution 3: Each support must support half the load if the beam is symmetrical. Reaction at each support = 500 N / 2 = 250 N.

Solution 4: The internal normal force in the rod at any section would also be 1000 N, assuming the rod is in tension and no other loads are present.

Solution 5: Centroid of a right triangle (from the base) = base/3 = 3 m / 3 = 1 m, height/3 = 4 m / 3 = 1.33 m.

Solution 6: Maximum static friction force = coefficient of static friction × normal force = 0.4 × 200 N = 80 N.

Solution 7: Free-body diagram should show the gravitational force acting downward through the center of mass, a normal force perpendicular to the slope, and a frictional force acting up the slope.

Solution 8: Weight = mass × gravitational acceleration = 10 kg × 9.81 m/s² = 98.1 N.

Solution 9: Normal force = Weight × cos(45 degrees) = 200 N × 0.707 = 141.4 N.

Solution 10: Moment of inertia (I) about the base = (base × height³) / 3 = (3 m × (2 m)³) / 3 = 24 m⁴ / 3 = 8 m⁴.

Chapter 9: Dynamics

Kinematics of Particles and Rigid Bodies

Kinematics is the branch of mechanics that deals with the motion of objects without considering the forces that cause this motion. It encompasses the study of the positions, velocities, and accelerations of objects and can be divided into the kinematics of particles — treating objects as mass points — and the kinematics of rigid bodies — where the object's rotation and translation are considered.

Principles of Kinematics

1. Kinematics of Particles: The kinematics of particles focuses on objects treated as single points where only translation is involved. This simplification is useful for analyzing the motion along a path, including straight-line motion and curvilinear motion.

- **Straight-line Motion:** Analyzed using equations that relate displacement, velocity, acceleration, and time without the need for direction considerations.

- **Curvilinear Motion:** Involves motion along a curved path where vector components of motion are considered in multiple dimensions, typically described in Cartesian, polar, or spherical coordinate systems.

2. Kinematics of Rigid Bodies: The study of rigid bodies involves both translational and rotational motion, adding complexity since the orientation of the body and its geometry affect the motion.

- **Translation:** All points on the rigid body have the same velocity and acceleration. The motion can be described similarly to particle kinematics but applied to the center of mass of the body.

- **Rotation:** Describes the angular motion about an axis. This includes angular velocity and angular acceleration, which describe how quickly an object rotates and how the rate of rotation changes over time, respectively.

- **General Plane Motion:** A combination of translation and rotation, where the body undergoes both movements simultaneously, such as a rolling wheel.

Equations and Concepts in Kinematics

1. Basic Equations: The fundamental equations used in the kinematics of particles and rigid bodies include:

- Velocity as the Derivative of Position: $v = \frac{ds}{dt}$ where s is the displacement.

- Acceleration as the Derivative of Velocity: $a = \frac{dv}{dt}$.

- Equations of Motion for Constant Acceleration: $v = v_0 + at$, $s = s_0 + v_0 t + \frac{1}{2}at^2$, and $v^2 = v_0^2 + 2a(s - s_0)$.

2. Angular Kinematics:

Key equations for angular motion include:

- Angular Velocity: $\omega = \frac{d\theta}{dt}$.
- Angular Acceleration: $\alpha = \frac{d\omega}{dt}$.
- Rotational Equations of Motion: Analogous to linear motion but applied to rotational movement.

Applications in Engineering

1. Vehicle Dynamics: Analyzing how vehicles accelerate and decelerate, understanding curvilinear paths for safety and efficiency in road design.

2. Robotics: Designing robotic arms and mechanisms that require precise movement and coordination between translation and rotation.

3. Aerospace Engineering: Studying the trajectory and orientation of aircraft and spacecraft, where both translational and angular motions are critical.

Challenges in Kinematics

1. Complexity of Motion: Real-world applications often involve complex motions that can be challenging to model and predict accurately, requiring advanced mathematics and computational tools.

2. Dealing with Non-Ideal Conditions: Friction, air resistance, and other forces can complicate kinematic analyses, necessitating the use of dynamics to fully understand the system's behavior.

3. Integration of Data: Accurate motion analysis often requires integration of data from various sensors and systems, presenting challenges in data compatibility and synchronization.

Conclusion

Understanding the kinematics of particles and rigid bodies forms the foundation for analyzing and designing systems in many areas of engineering. By mastering these concepts, engineers can predict and optimize the behavior of various mechanical systems, enhancing their functionality and effectiveness in real-world applications. The study of kinematics not only supports engineering designs but also fosters a deeper understanding of the fundamental principles governing motion in the physical world.

Linear and Angular Motion

Linear and angular motions are fundamental concepts in the study of dynamics, essential for understanding how objects move in space. Linear motion pertains to the movement of objects along a straight or curved path, while angular motion refers to the rotation of objects around an axis. Both types of motion are crucial in a variety of engineering applications, from the design of simple mechanical systems to complex aerospace structures.

Principles of Linear Motion

1. **Displacement, Velocity, and Acceleration:**
   - **Displacement** is a vector quantity that represents the change in position of an object.
   - **Velocity** is the rate of change of displacement and is a vector quantity that indicates the direction and speed of motion.
   - **Acceleration** is the rate of change of velocity, indicating how velocity changes with time.

2. **Equations of Motion:**

The basic equations governing linear motion for constant acceleration include:

- $v = v_0 + at$
- $s = s_0 + v_0 t + \frac{1}{2}at^2$
- $v^2 = v_0^2 + 2a(s - s_0)$

    where v is velocity, s is displacement, a is acceleration, t is time, and subscript 0 denotes initial conditions.

Principles of Angular Motion

1. **Angular Displacement, Velocity, and Acceleration:**
   - **Angular Displacement** is the angle through which an object moves about a fixed axis.
   - **Angular Velocity** is the rate of change of angular displacement and describes how quickly an object rotates.
   - **Angular Acceleration** is the rate of change of angular velocity.

2. **Rotational Equations of Motion:**

Similar to linear motion, the equations for constant angular acceleration are:

- $\omega = \omega_0 + \alpha t$
- $\theta = \theta_0 + \omega_0 t + \frac{1}{2}\alpha t^2$
- $\omega^2 = \omega_0^2 + 2\alpha(\theta - \theta_0)$

    where ω is angular velocity, θ is angular displacement, α is angular acceleration, and t is time.

Relationship Between Linear and Angular Motion

In many engineering systems, linear and angular motions are interconnected, particularly in mechanisms involving rotation, such as gears, wheels, and pulleys. The relationship can be expressed through:

- $v = r\omega$
- $a_{tangential} = r\alpha$

  where r is the radius of the path of the motion or the distance from the axis of rotation to the point of interest.

Applications in Engineering

1. Mechanical Systems: Understanding both linear and angular motion is essential for designing mechanical systems that involve elements like cams, cranks, pistons, and flywheels, which convert between rotational and translational motion.

2. Robotics: Robots often require precise control of both linear and angular movement to perform tasks accurately, whether in assembly lines or for complex surgeries.

3. Automotive and Aerospace: In automotive engineering, the dynamics of the vehicle's tires involve understanding the translation of rotational motion into linear motion. In aerospace, angular motion principles help in stabilizing and maneuvering aircraft.

Challenges in Analyzing Linear and Angular Motion

1. Complex Systems Interaction: Many systems involve complex interactions between linear and angular motions which can be challenging to model and analyze accurately without advanced simulation tools.

2. Non-uniform Accelerations: Dealing with varying accelerations due to forces such as friction, air resistance, or gravitational variations requires intricate differential equations and numerical methods.

3. Measurement and Data Accuracy: Accurately measuring and interpreting motion parameters like displacement, velocity, and acceleration in both linear and angular forms can be challenging, particularly at high speeds or over small scales.

Conclusion

Linear and angular motions are cornerstones of dynamic analysis in physics and engineering. Mastery of these concepts allows engineers to design more efficient, safer, and innovative machines and structures. Understanding these types of motion not only enhances the functionality and performance of mechanical systems but also contributes to advancements in technology and industry.

Impulse and Momentum

Impulse and momentum are foundational concepts in dynamics, crucial for analyzing the behavior of objects in motion. Momentum is a measure of the motion of an object and is conserved in isolated systems, while impulse describes the change in momentum caused by a force over a time interval. Understanding these principles is essential for solving problems related to collisions, explosions, and other dynamic events in engineering and physics.

Definitions and Principles

1. Momentum:

Momentum ($\vec{p}$) is a vector quantity defined as the product of an object's mass (m) and its velocity ($\vec{v}$). It is expressed as:

$$\vec{p} = m\vec{v}$$

Momentum is conserved in the absence of external forces, meaning that the total momentum of a closed system remains constant regardless of the interactions within the system.

2. Impulse:

Impulse ($\vec{J}$) is also a vector quantity and is defined as the integral of force ($\vec{F}$) over the time interval (Δt) during which the force acts. It is given by:

$$\vec{J} = \int \vec{F}\, dt$$

Impulse is equal to the change in momentum of an object:

$$\vec{J} = \Delta \vec{p} = m\Delta \vec{v}$$

Applications of Impulse and Momentum

1. Collision Analysis: In collision dynamics, whether elastic or inelastic, conservation of momentum is a key tool for determining the post-collision velocities of colliding bodies when combined with energy conservation principles.

2. Sports Mechanics: Impulse and momentum play critical roles in sports. For example, the way a bat strikes a ball, transferring momentum and generating impulse, determines the speed and direction of the ball.

3. Vehicle Safety: In automotive engineering, understanding impulse and momentum is vital for designing safety features like airbags and crumple zones that effectively manage the forces during a crash, minimizing injury by extending the time over which the impulse acts.

Mathematical Formulations

1. Conservation of Momentum: For a system of particles, the total momentum before and after an event (like a collision) is the same if no external forces act on the system:

$$\sum \vec{p}_{\text{initial}} = \sum \vec{p}_{\text{final}}$$

2. Calculating Impulse:

Impulse can be calculated from force-time graphs as the area under the force curve:

$$\vec{J} = \int_{t_1}^{t_2} \vec{F}\, dt$$

This formulation is particularly useful in scenarios where force varies over time.

Challenges in Practical Applications

1. Complex Systems: In multi-body systems, especially where interactions are not limited to linear or planar movements, calculating the changes in momentum and the corresponding impulses can become highly complex.

2. Variable Forces: When forces vary unpredictably over time or depend on the velocity or position of the bodies involved, integrating these forces to find impulse requires advanced calculus and sometimes numerical methods.

3. External Influences: In real-world applications, external forces such as friction, air resistance, or gravitational variations can affect the conservation of momentum, requiring adjustments to the basic theoretical models.

Conclusion

Impulse and momentum are crucial in understanding the dynamics of moving objects. These concepts not only allow engineers to predict and analyze the motion of objects under various force conditions but also enable the design of systems and devices that can control or utilize these forces effectively. Mastery of impulse and momentum is essential for engineers across disciplines, including mechanical, aerospace, automotive, and civil engineering, providing the tools to solve complex dynamic problems and innovate in the design of technology and machinery.

Work, Energy, and Power

Work, energy, and power are fundamental concepts in the field of dynamics, providing a framework for understanding how forces cause motion and how that motion is sustained and transferred. These principles are critical in analyzing mechanical systems, designing energy-efficient machines, and solving problems related to mechanical performance and efficiency.

Definitions and Basic Principles

1. Work: Work is defined as the force exerted on an object causing it to move. The work done by a force is the product of the force and the displacement of the object in the direction of the force:

$$W = \vec{F} \cdot \vec{d} = Fd\cos(\theta)$$

where W is work, $\vec{F}$ is force, $\vec{d}$ is displacement, and θ is the angle between the force and displacement vectors.

2. Energy:

Energy is the capacity to do work. In dynamics, mechanical energy is typically considered, which can be:

- Kinetic Energy (KE): Energy an object possesses due to its motion, given by $KE = \frac{1}{2}mv^2$ where m is mass and v is velocity.

- Potential Energy (PE): Energy stored in an object due to its position or configuration, such as gravitational potential energy $PE = mgh$ where g is the acceleration due to gravity and h is the height above a reference point.

3. Power:

Power is the rate at which work is done or energy is transferred. It is defined as:

$$P = \frac{W}{t}$$

where P is power, W is work, and t is time. In terms of force and velocity, power can also be expressed as $P = \vec{F} \cdot \vec{v}$.

Applications in Engineering

1. Mechanical Design: Understanding work and energy principles is essential for designing mechanical systems such as engines, turbines, and pumps, where efficiency in energy transfer is crucial.

2. Automotive Engineering: In automotive engineering, the concepts of work, energy, and power are applied to optimize the performance and fuel efficiency of vehicles.

3. Renewable Energy Systems: In the design and evaluation of renewable energy systems, such as wind turbines and solar panels, power calculations are fundamental to determining the output and efficiency of energy conversion systems.

Analyzing Work, Energy, and Power

1. Work-Energy Principle: The work-energy principle states that the work done by all forces acting on a particle equals the change in its kinetic energy:

$$W_{\text{total}} = \Delta KE$$

This principle is a powerful tool for analyzing the motion of objects without explicitly dealing with the forces involved.

2. Conservation of Mechanical Energy: In the absence of non-conservative forces (like friction or air resistance), the total mechanical energy (kinetic + potential) of a system remains constant. This principle simplifies the analysis of many mechanical systems, particularly in conservative fields.

3. Calculating Power in Variable Systems: In systems where force or velocity changes over time, power calculation requires integration:

$$P(t) = \vec{F}(t) \cdot \vec{v}(t)$$

This can be used to analyze varying loads in machinery and dynamic responses in vehicles.

Challenges in Practical Applications

1. Non-Conservative Forces: Accounting for energy losses due to non-conservative forces like friction or drag adds complexity to energy calculations, requiring more detailed analysis to ensure accuracy.

2. Real-Time Monitoring and Control: In systems where real-time energy efficiency is critical, continuous monitoring of power and energy metrics is challenging but necessary for optimal performance.

3. Scalability of Systems: Scaling up mechanical systems often introduces non-linearities in energy dynamics, making direct scaling of work, energy, and power calculations non-trivial.

Conclusion

Work, energy, and power are indispensable concepts in dynamics, deeply intertwined with the design and analysis of virtually all mechanical systems. A thorough understanding of these principles not only enables engineers to design more effective and efficient machines but also contributes to innovations in energy conservation and management. Mastery of these topics is essential for advancing technology in ways that are sustainable and responsive to the growing global demand for energy solutions.

Dynamic Friction

Dynamic friction, also known as kinetic friction, is the force that opposes the relative motion between two bodies in contact. It acts tangentially to the surfaces in contact and plays a critical role in various engineering and physical scenarios, from automotive braking systems to the motion of machinery. Understanding dynamic friction is crucial for accurately predicting and controlling the movement of objects under external forces.

Fundamentals of Dynamic Friction

1. Definition and Characteristics: Dynamic friction occurs when two surfaces are sliding against each other and is generally less than static friction, which acts when there is no relative motion. Dynamic friction remains approximately constant regardless of the speed of sliding, but it depends on the nature of the surfaces and the normal force pressing them together.

2. Coefficient of Dynamic Friction (μk): The coefficient of dynamic friction is a dimensionless number that describes the ratio of the force of friction between two bodies and the force pressing them together. This coefficient is determined empirically through experimentation and is specific to the pair of materials in contact.

Mathematical Description

1. Frictional Force Equation: The force of dynamic friction (Fk) can be expressed by the equation:

$$F_k = \mu_k N$$

where μ_k is the coefficient of dynamic friction and N is the normal force perpendicular to the contact surface.

2. Factors Influencing Dynamic Friction:

- **Material Properties:** Different materials have different inherent roughness and adhesive characteristics, affecting μk.

- **Surface Conditions:** Lubrication, surface roughness, and contaminants can alter the level of friction encountered.

- **Normal Force:** Increasing the normal force increases the frictional force linearly, assuming the coefficient of dynamic friction remains constant.

Applications of Dynamic Friction

1. Automotive Systems: In vehicles, dynamic friction is crucial for the effectiveness of braking systems. The friction between brake pads and discs or drums converts kinetic energy into thermal energy, slowing the vehicle.

2. Manufacturing and Machinery: Dynamic friction affects the operation of moving mechanical assemblies. Proper management of friction through lubricants can prevent wear and tear, reduce energy consumption, and prolong equipment life.

3. Sports and Recreation: Dynamic friction influences the performance of athletes and the design of sports equipment, from the grip of athletic shoes on various surfaces to the sliding of skis on snow.

Analyzing Dynamic Friction

1. Energy Considerations: The work done against frictional force is transformed into heat, affecting the thermal energy balance of the systems involved. The energy dissipated can be calculated by:

$$W = F_k \cdot d$$

where d is the distance over which the friction acts.

2. System Dynamics: Dynamic friction must be accounted for in the equations of motion for systems undergoing sliding or rolling, impacting acceleration and velocity.

Challenges in Dynamic Friction

1. Variable Conditions: Friction coefficients can vary with changes in speed, temperature, and wear, making it difficult to predict friction accurately in dynamic situations.

2. Measurement and Control: Accurately measuring dynamic friction in real-time is challenging, especially in complex systems. Controlling it requires precise engineering and often sophisticated feedback systems.

3. Heat Generation: Frictional heating can lead to thermal expansion or damage. Managing this heat is critical in high-speed machinery and braking systems.

Conclusion

Dynamic friction is a pivotal factor in the analysis and design of any system involving relative motion between surfaces. It affects not only the operational efficiency and energy consumption of mechanical systems but also safety and functionality. Understanding and accurately predicting dynamic friction are essential for engineers to design more reliable, efficient, and effective mechanical systems and devices.

Vibrations

Vibrations refer to the oscillatory motion of physical systems, ranging from simple pendulums to complex structures like bridges and skyscrapers, as well as critical components in mechanical and aerospace engineering such as engines and spacecraft. Understanding vibrations is essential for designing systems that can withstand or exploit these movements, ensuring stability, longevity, and functionality.

Fundamental Concepts of Vibrations

1. **Types of Vibrations:**

    - **Free Vibrations:** Occur without external forces acting on the system, driven solely by the system's initial energy.
    - **Forced Vibrations:** Result from external forces that drive the system at a frequency that may or may not match the system's natural frequency.
    - **Damped Vibrations:** Involve energy loss from the system over time due to resistive forces like friction or air resistance, leading to a gradual decrease in amplitude.

2. **Key Parameters:**

    - **Natural Frequency:** The frequency at which a system tends to oscillate in the absence of any driving or damping force.
    - **Damping Ratio:** A dimensionless measure describing how oscillations in a system decay after a disturbance.
    - **Amplitude:** The maximum extent of a vibration or oscillation, measured from the position of equilibrium.

Mathematical Modeling of Vibrations

1. Simple Harmonic Motion (SHM): The simplest type of vibration can be modeled as SHM, where the restoring force is directly proportional to the displacement and acts in the direction opposite to that of displacement. The equation of motion for a simple harmonic oscillator is:

$$m\ddot{x} + kx = 0$$

where m is mass, $\ddot{x}$ is the acceleration, x is the displacement, and k is the spring constant.

2. Damping and Energy Dissipation: For damped vibrations, the equation of motion includes a damping term:

$$m\ddot{x} + c\dot{x} + kx = 0$$

where c is the damping coefficient and $\dot{x}$ is the velocity.

3. Response to Periodic Forcing: When a system is subjected to a periodic force, the steady-state solution of the motion equation can be complex, particularly near resonance, where the driving frequency is close to the system's natural frequency. The equation is:

$$m\ddot{x} + c\dot{x} + kx = F_0 \cos(\omega t)$$

where F_0 is the amplitude of the external force and ω is its frequency.

Applications of Vibration Analysis

1. Engineering Design: Vibrations analysis is critical in engineering to ensure that structures and mechanical components can endure operational and environmental vibrations without failure.

2. Earthquake Engineering: Buildings and other structures are designed considering their natural frequencies to avoid resonance with earthquake ground motions.

3. Noise Reduction: In automotive and aerospace industries, reducing vibrations is key to decreasing noise levels, which enhances comfort and compliance with regulatory standards.

Challenges in Vibrations

1. Predicting Complex Interactions: Real-world systems often involve nonlinear interactions and coupled modes of vibrations that can be challenging to predict and require sophisticated computational methods.

2. Measurement and Control: Accurately measuring vibrations, especially in hostile environments like engines or during rocket launches, is technically demanding. Controlling unwanted vibrations often requires active or passive systems that introduce additional complexity and cost.

3. Material Fatigue and Failure: Repeated stress from vibrations can lead to material fatigue and structural failure, necessitating detailed analysis and robust design to ensure longevity.

Conclusion

Vibrations are a pervasive aspect of many mechanical systems and structures, influencing design, operation, and maintenance decisions. Mastery of vibration analysis enables engineers to create safer, more efficient, and more resilient designs. Understanding and effectively managing vibrations not only enhances the performance and safety of engineered systems but also contributes to innovation in technology development and implementation.

Problems:

Problem 1: Kinematics of Particles Calculate the final velocity of a particle that starts from rest and accelerates uniformly at 2 m/s² over a distance of 50 meters.

Problem 2: Linear Motion A car accelerates from 0 to 60 km/h in 5 seconds. What is the average acceleration in m/s²?

Problem 3: Angular Motion Determine the angular velocity of a wheel that rotates 30 revolutions in 10 seconds.

Problem 4: Impulse and Momentum A 5 kg object moving at 10 m/s receives an impulse of 15 N·s. What is the object's final velocity?

Problem 5: Work, Energy, and Power How much work is done by a force of 10 N moving an object 3 meters in the direction of the force?

Problem 6: Dynamic Friction If the coefficient of dynamic friction between a sliding box and the ground is 0.3, and the normal force is 150 N, what is the frictional force acting on the box?

Problem 7: Vibrations A mass-spring system has a mass of 2 kg and a spring constant of 200 N/m. What is the natural frequency of the system?

Problem 8: Kinematics of Rigid Bodies Calculate the velocity of a point on a rotating rigid body at a radius of 0.5 meters from the center if the body has an angular speed of 20 rad/s.

Problem 9: Work, Energy, and Power What is the kinetic energy of a 100 kg object moving at a velocity of 5 m/s?

Problem 10: Impulse and Momentum A ball of mass 0.2 kg moving at 2 m/s collides with a wall and rebounds at the same speed. What is the change in momentum?

Solutions:

Solution 1:
$$v^2 = v_0^2 + 2a \cdot s$$
$$v^2 = 0 + 2 \cdot 2 \cdot 50 = 200$$
$$v = \sqrt{200} \approx 14.14 \, \text{m/s}$$

Solution 2:
$$v = 60 \, \text{km/h} = 16.67 \, \text{m/s}$$
$$a = \frac{\Delta v}{\Delta t} = \frac{16.67}{5} = 3.33 \, \text{m/s}^2$$

Solution 3:
$\omega = \frac{2\pi \cdot N}{t} = \frac{2\pi \cdot 30}{10} = 6\pi \text{ rad/s} \approx 18.85 \text{ rad/s}$

Solution 4:
$\Delta v = \frac{J}{m} = \frac{15}{5} = 3 \text{ m/s}$
$v_f = v_i + \Delta v = 10 + 3 = 13 \text{ m/s}$

Solution 5:
$W = F \cdot d \cdot \cos(\theta) = 10 \cdot 3 \cdot 1 = 30 \text{ J}$

Solution 6:
$F_f = \mu_k \cdot N = 0.3 \cdot 150 = 45 \text{ N}$

Solution 7:
$\omega_n = \sqrt{\frac{k}{m}} = \sqrt{\frac{200}{2}} = 10 \text{ rad/s}$

Solution 8:
$v = r \cdot \omega = 0.5 \cdot 20 = 10 \text{ m/s}$

Solution 9:
$KE = \frac{1}{2} m v^2 = \frac{1}{2} \cdot 100 \cdot 5^2 = 1250 \text{ J}$

Solution 10:
$\Delta p = m \cdot (-v - v) = 0.2 \cdot (-2 - 2) = -0.8 \text{ kg m/s}$
(Note: Negative sign indicates a change in direction.)

Chapter 10: Strength of Materials

Stress and Strain Types

Stress and strain are fundamental concepts in the field of materials science and structural engineering, describing how materials deform under various loads. Understanding different types of stress and strain is crucial for designing safe and efficient structures and machinery that can withstand operational and environmental demands without failure.

Definitions and Basic Principles

1. Stress: Stress (σ) is defined as the internal force divided by the area over which the force is applied, typically measured in pascals (Pa) or pounds per square inch (psi). Stress describes the intensity of the internal forces acting within a deformable body.

2. Strain: Strain (ϵ) is a measure of deformation representing the displacement between particles in the body relative to a reference length. Strain is a dimensionless number, indicating how much an object is stretched or compressed as a result of an applied load.

Types of Stress

1. Normal Stress:

- **Tensile Stress:** Occurs when forces act to elongate the material, pulling apart the particles within the material.
- **Compressive Stress:** Occurs when forces act to compress or shorten the material.

2. Shear Stress: Shear stress occurs when forces are applied in opposite directions on either side of a material, causing the particles within the material to slide past each other. It is common in fasteners like bolts and rivets, as well as in beams subjected to transverse loads.

3. Bearing Stress: Bearing stress is a type of stress that occurs when a force is applied over a small area, such as when a structural component rests on another, transferring the load via contact pressure.

Types of Strain

1. Axial Strain: Occurs when a material deforms along its length. In tension or compression, axial strain is calculated as the change in length divided by the original length.

2. Shear Strain: Occurs when the material is subjected to shear stress, causing a change in angle between lines originally perpendicular to each other within the material.

3. Volumetric Strain: The change in volume of a material divided by its original volume, usually under the action of compressive stress.

Stress-Strain Relationship

The relationship between stress and strain is typically characterized by the material's stress-strain curve, which is obtained from tensile tests. Key points on this curve include:

- **Proportional Limit:** The highest stress at which stress is directly proportional to strain, following Hooke's Law ($\sigma = E\epsilon$), where E is the Young's modulus.
- **Elastic Limit:** The maximum stress that a material can withstand without permanent deformation.
- **Yield Point:** The stress at which a material begins to deform plastically, and beyond which deformation will be permanent.
- **Ultimate Strength:** The maximum stress on the stress-strain curve, representing the maximum stress material can withstand.
- **Fracture Point:** The stress at which a material ultimately fails and breaks.

Applications and Importance in Engineering

1. Structural Engineering: Knowing the different types of stress and how materials respond helps in designing buildings, bridges, and other structures to ensure they can endure loads without excessive deformation or failure.

2. Mechanical Engineering: In mechanical systems, understanding stress and strain guides the design of components like shafts, gears, and bearings that are subject to various loads during operation.

3. Aerospace Engineering: Stress and strain analysis is critical for the design of aircraft components, which must withstand high levels of tensile and shear stress while minimizing weight.

Challenges in Stress and Strain Analysis

1. Complex Loadings: Real-world applications often involve complex combinations of different types of stress, requiring sophisticated analysis methods to accurately predict material behavior.

2. Material Anisotropy: Materials like composites exhibit different properties in different directions, complicating stress and strain predictions.

3. Temperature Effects: Temperature changes can significantly affect material strength and deformation characteristics, adding another layer of complexity to stress and strain analysis.

Conclusion

Understanding the various types of stress and strain is essential for engineers across all disciplines. This knowledge allows for the design and analysis of materials and structures to ensure safety, functionality, and durability. Advanced understanding of these concepts leads to innovative engineering solutions capable of overcoming some of the most challenging design problems.

Combined Loading

Combined loading refers to the situation where a structural element or material is subjected to multiple types of loads simultaneously, such as bending, axial, shear, and torsional loads. This complex interplay of forces is common in engineering practice, demanding thorough analysis to ensure structural integrity and safety.

Fundamentals of Combined Loading

1. **Types of Loads in Combined Loading:**

    - **Axial Loads:** Forces applied along the length of an element, causing tensile or compressive stress.
    - **Shear Loads:** Forces that cause one part of a material to slide over another, generating shear stress.
    - **Bending Loads:** Moments that induce bending stress within an element, typically in beams.
    - **Torsional Loads:** Twisting forces that produce torsional stress, particularly in cylindrical shafts or similar components.

2. **Stress Superposition:** In combined loading scenarios, the total stress experienced by a material at any point is the algebraic sum of the stresses due to each type of load. This principle of superposition is fundamental in analyzing complex loading situations.

Analyzing Combined Loading

1. **Stress Analysis:** To determine the total stress under combined loading:

$$\sigma_{total} = \sigma_{axial} + \sigma_{bending} + \sigma_{shear}$$

where each stress component is calculated based on the specific loading conditions and the geometry of the structural element.

2. **Strain Compatibility:** When multiple loads are applied, the material must deform in a manner that is compatible with all loading types. This concept ensures that the strain calculations are consistent across the different modes of loading.

3. **Failure Criteria:** Assessing the safety of structures under combined loading involves using failure theories appropriate for the material, such as:

    - **Maximum Normal Stress Theory:** Suitable for brittle materials.
    - **Maximum Shear Stress Theory:** Often used for ductile materials.
    - **Von Mises Stress Criterion:** A more generalized approach used for predicting yield in ductile materials under complex loading states.

Practical Applications and Considerations

1. **Structural Engineering:** Beams in buildings and bridges often experience combined bending and axial loads, especially in elements that support uneven loads or are subjected to wind or seismic forces.

2. **Mechanical Engineering:** Shafts in machinery may experience torsion from rotational mechanisms while also bearing axial loads from weights or other components.

3. **Aerospace Engineering:** Aircraft wings undergo complex loading combinations including bending from aerodynamic forces and torsion from maneuvering which must be meticulously analyzed to prevent failure.

Computational Methods in Combined Loading Analysis

1. Finite Element Analysis (FEA): FEA is a powerful computational tool used to analyze complex combined loading situations by breaking down the structure into smaller, manageable elements, allowing detailed visualization and analysis of stress and strain distribution.

2. Experimental Stress Analysis: Techniques like photoelasticity or strain gauging are used to validate theoretical predictions and ensure that the components can withstand the combined loads in real-world applications.

Challenges in Combined Loading

1. Complexity of Analysis: The interaction of different types of loads can lead to stress concentrations and complex deformation patterns that are challenging to predict accurately.

2. Material Behavior: Materials may exhibit different properties under different loading conditions, making it essential to understand the material characteristics thoroughly.

3. Scale and Environment Effects: In large-scale structures or components operating under varying environmental conditions, combined loads can lead to unexpected responses, necessitating robust design and testing protocols.

Conclusion

Understanding and effectively analyzing combined loading are crucial for the safety and functionality of engineering structures and components. Engineers must employ a mix of theoretical knowledge, computational tools, and experimental methods to ensure that designs can withstand the complex interactions of multiple loads. Mastery of combined loading analysis not only enhances the reliability of structures but also pushes the boundaries of what can be achieved in modern engineering designs.

Beam, Truss, Frame, and Column Analysis

Analysis of beams, trusses, frames, and columns is pivotal in structural engineering, providing the foundation for designing buildings, bridges, and other structures. Each type of member has specific roles and behaviors under loads, and understanding these characteristics is essential for ensuring stability, durability, and safety in construction.

Beam Analysis

1. Types of Beams:

- **Simply Supported Beams:** Supported at both ends with reactions that can resist vertical forces but not moments.
- **Cantilever Beams:** Fixed at one end and free at the other, bearing bending moments and shear forces along their length.
- **Continuous Beams:** Span over more than two supports, offering greater stability and load distribution.

2. Load Types and Effects:

- **Point Loads:** Concentrated forces that cause bending at the application point.

- **Distributed Loads:** Spread across a length of the beam, causing bending and shear variations along the beam.

3. Bending Moment and Shear Force: Understanding the bending moment and shear force distributions along a beam is crucial for determining the maximum stresses and deflections, using the relationships:

- $V = \frac{dM}{dx}$
- $\frac{dV}{dx} = -w$

  where V is shear force, M is bending moment, w is load per unit length, and x is the position along the beam.

Truss Analysis

1. Assumptions for Trusses:

- Members are connected at joints considered as pin connections.
- Loads and reactions are applied only at the joints.
- Members carry only axial forces (tension or compression).

2. Method of Joints: This method involves isolating a joint to find the forces in the connected members, using equilibrium equations

$(\Sigma F_x = 0, \Sigma F_y = 0)$ for each joint.

3. Method of Sections: This method involves cutting through some members of the truss to form a section and analyzing the section as a free body to determine the forces in the cut members.

Frame Analysis

1. Characteristics of Frames:

- Frames are structures with at least one multi-force member (beam or column), designed to support loads and resist moments.
- Unlike trusses, frames undergo bending along with axial deformation.

2. Load Types and Analysis: Frame analysis often requires considering bending moments, axial forces, and shear forces simultaneously, using methods similar to those for beams but accounting for the additional complexity of multiple connections and variable member orientations.

Column Analysis

1. Buckling and Stability: Columns primarily carry axial compressive loads and are susceptible to buckling under critical loads. Euler's formula for buckling load is given by:

- $P_{cr} = \frac{\pi^2 EI}{(KL)^2}$

  where E is the modulus of elasticity, I is the moment of inertia of the column cross-section, L is the effective length, and K is the column effective length factor.

2. Slenderness Ratio:

The slenderness ratio ($\lambda = \frac{KL}{r}$) of a column, where r is the radius of gyration, affects its susceptibility to buckling. Columns with higher slenderness ratios are more prone to buckling.

Challenges in Structural Analysis

1. Material Properties and Load Assumptions: Accurate knowledge of material properties and realistic assumptions about load types and distributions are critical for reliable analysis.

2. Geometric Nonlinearities: Large deformations can introduce nonlinear behavior in structural members, complicating analysis and requiring more sophisticated methods.

3. Connection Details: The behavior of structural systems can significantly depend on the design of connections (rigid, pinned, or semi-rigid), influencing the overall response of the structure.

Conclusion

The analysis of beams, trusses, frames, and columns is central to the field of civil and structural engineering. Mastery of the methods and principles used to analyze these elements allows engineers to design structures that are not only efficient and economical but also meet safety standards and resist environmental and operational loads effectively. Understanding the complexities and interdependencies of different structural components ensures the integrity and longevity of engineering projects.

Shear and Moment Diagrams

Shear and moment diagrams are essential tools in structural engineering, used to represent how internal shear forces and bending moments vary along the length of a beam or other structural elements under load. These diagrams are crucial for the design and analysis of beams and other structural members to ensure they can withstand applied loads without failing.

Fundamentals of Shear and Moment Diagrams

1. Shear Force Diagram (SFD): A shear force diagram shows the variation of shear force (V) along the length of a beam. The shear force at any section of a beam is a result of the transverse loads (such as point loads, distributed loads, and reactions) applied to the beam.

2. Bending Moment Diagram (BMD): A bending moment diagram displays the bending moment (M) acting at various sections of the beam. The bending moment is the result of forces causing the beam to bend, reflecting the moment's tendency to rotate sections of the beam about a centroidal axis.

Constructing Shear and Moment Diagrams

1. Determining Support Reactions: The first step in constructing shear and moment diagrams is to calculate the reactions at supports using static equilibrium equations $(\Sigma F_x = 0, \Sigma F_y = 0, \Sigma M = 0)$.

2. Plotting Shear Force Diagrams:

- Start from one end of the beam (usually the left).
- Add up the vertical forces (upwards positive and downwards negative).
- The value of shear force changes abruptly at the point of application of concentrated loads.
- The shear force remains constant between loads and varies linearly with distributed loads.

3. Plotting Bending Moment Diagrams:

- The moment diagram is related to the shear diagram as the integral of the shear force along the length of the beam.
- Bending moments change where shear forces are non-zero and remain constant where shear is zero.
- Points of zero shear are potential locations for maximum or minimum moments.

4. Relationships and Conventions:

- $\frac{dV}{dx} = -w$ (where w is the load per unit length, indicating how shear force changes under distributed loads).
- $\frac{dM}{dx} = V$ (this relationship shows that the slope of the moment diagram at any point is equal to the shear force at that point).

Applications of Shear and Moment Diagrams

1. Beam Design and Analysis: Engineers use shear and moment diagrams to determine the maximum shear forces and bending moments to select appropriate beam sizes, materials, and reinforcements to ensure safety and efficiency.

2. Load Optimization: These diagrams help in optimizing the placement of loads and the design of beam supports to minimize material usage while enhancing structural integrity.

3. Failure Prediction: Identifying points of maximum stress using moment diagrams allows engineers to predict potential failure points, which is crucial for safety assessments and inspections.

Challenges in Shear and Moment Diagrams

1. Complex Loadings and Supports: Diagrams become complex with the presence of varying types of loads (point, distributed, varying distributed) and support conditions (fixed, pinned, sliding), requiring meticulous calculations and often computational assistance.

2. Non-Prismatic Beams: For beams that change cross-sectional area along their length, shear and moment calculations are more complex and require more detailed analysis.

3. Dynamic Loading: When beams are subjected to dynamic or moving loads, shear and moment diagrams need to account for the varying location and magnitude of these loads over time.

Conclusion

Shear and moment diagrams are indispensable in structural engineering, providing critical insights into force distributions within beams and other structural members. Mastery of these diagrams enables engineers to design safer and more efficient structures by precisely understanding and addressing the stresses and forces within them. As engineering challenges grow more complex, the ability to accurately generate and interpret these diagrams remains a fundamental skill in the engineer's toolkit.

Material Failure Theories

Material failure theories are crucial for predicting when and how materials will fail under various loading conditions. These theories help engineers design safer, more reliable structures and components by understanding the limits of material strength and the mechanics of failure. Each theory provides a different perspective on failure, applicable under specific conditions or for particular materials.

Fundamental Concepts of Material Failure

1. Stress State: Material failure theories often depend on the stress state within the material, which may include uniaxial, biaxial, or triaxial stress conditions. Understanding the stress state is crucial for applying the correct failure theory.

2. Failure Criteria: Failure criteria are conditions under which a material is predicted to fail. These criteria vary depending on the material (ductile or brittle) and the type of stress (tensile, compressive, shear).

Key Material Failure Theories

1. Maximum Normal Stress Theory (Rankine's Theory): Applicable primarily to brittle materials, this theory posits that failure occurs when the maximum normal stress in the material exceeds the ultimate tensile or compressive strength. It does not consider the effect of shear stress.

2. Maximum Shear Stress Theory (Tresca Criterion): Often used for ductile materials, this theory states that failure occurs when the maximum shear stress in the material reaches the shear strength of the material as determined by a shear test. This theory is particularly relevant for predicting yield failure in metals.

3. Distortion Energy Theory (Von Mises Criterion): This theory is widely used for ductile materials under complex loading conditions. It suggests that failure occurs when the distortion energy per unit volume due to applied stresses reaches the distortion energy per unit volume at yield in a simple tension test. It provides a more accurate prediction in multiaxial stress conditions compared to the Tresca Criterion.

4. Mohr-Coulomb Theory: Commonly used in geotechnical engineering for soils and rocks, this theory combines the effects of normal and shear stress and posits that failure occurs along a plane where the shear stress exceeds the material's cohesive strength, modified by the effect of internal friction dependent on the normal stress on the plane.

Applications of Material Failure Theories

1. Structural Engineering: Understanding how materials fail under different loads allows for the design of buildings and bridges that can withstand expected stressors without collapsing.

2. Mechanical Components: In mechanical engineering, components are often designed using failure theories to ensure that they do not fail under operational stresses, including those encountered in automotive and aerospace applications.

3. Earthquake and Geotechnical Design: Material failure theories are essential in designing structures that interact with soil and rock, where failure conditions are often complex due to varied loads during events like earthquakes.

Challenges in Applying Material Failure Theories

1. Complexity of Real-World Conditions: Real-world conditions often involve complex loading scenarios that are not purely uniaxial or simple. Accurately modeling these conditions and applying failure theories correctly requires sophisticated analysis tools and deep understanding.

2. Material Heterogeneity: Materials are not always homogeneous and isotropic. Local defects, anisotropy, and variations in properties can affect failure predictions, necessitating more detailed analysis and often material-specific testing.

3. Dynamic and Fatigue Loading: Many failures occur under dynamic or cyclic loading conditions that are not covered by static failure theories. Fatigue and impact loadings require separate analyses to predict failure accurately.

Conclusion

Material failure theories are integral to the design process in engineering, providing the basis for predicting when materials will fail and under what conditions. Mastery of these theories enables engineers to enhance the safety and reliability of structures and components across a range of applications. Understanding how to apply these theories effectively in the context of modern engineering challenges continues to be a crucial area of research and development in materials science and engineering disciplines.

Problems:

Problem 1: Stress Types Calculate the normal stress in a steel rod with a diameter of 10 mm subjected to an axial tensile load of 5,000 N.

Problem 2: Combined Loading Determine the equivalent stress at a point on a shaft that is subjected to an axial tension of 100 kN and a torque of 500 N·m.

Problem 3: Beam Analysis A simply supported beam with a length of 6 m carries a uniformly distributed load of 2 kN/m. Calculate the maximum bending moment.

Problem 4: Truss Analysis For a truss joint where two members, each carrying 5 kN, meet at an angle of 90 degrees, find the resultant force.

Problem 5: Frame Analysis Determine the horizontal shear force at the base of a fixed-frame subjected to a horizontal load of 10 kN at its top.

Problem 6: Column Buckling Calculate the critical buckling load for a steel column that is 3 m long, with a moment of inertia of 80,000 mm^4, and a modulus of elasticity of 200 GPa.

Problem 7: Shear and Moment Diagrams Sketch the shear force diagram for a beam that is 4 m long with pinned supports at both ends and a point load of 10 kN at the midpoint.

Problem 8: Material Failure Theories Using the maximum shear stress theory, determine the safety factor for a material subjected to a plane stress condition with principal stresses of 100 MPa and -50 MPa, if the yield strength in shear is 60 MPa.

Problem 9: Dynamic Friction Calculate the dynamic friction force for an object weighing 200 N sliding over a horizontal surface with a coefficient of dynamic friction of 0.4.

Problem 10: Vibrations For a mass-spring system with a mass of 2 kg and a spring constant of 50 N/m, determine the natural frequency of vibration.

Solutions:

Solution 1:
$$\sigma = \frac{F}{A}$$
$$A = \frac{\pi d^2}{4} = \frac{\pi (0.01)^2}{4} = 7.854 \times 10^{-5}\, m^2$$
$$\sigma = \frac{5000}{7.854 \times 10^{-5}} = 63.66\, MPa$$

Solution 2:
$$\tau = \frac{T}{J}$$
$$J = \frac{\pi d^4}{32} = \frac{\pi (0.1)^4}{32} = 3.07 \times 10^{-5}\, m^4$$
$$\tau = \frac{500}{3.07 \times 10^{-5}} = 16.29\, MPa$$
$$\sigma_{equivalent} = \sqrt{\sigma^2 + 3\tau^2} = \sqrt{(100)^2 + 3(16.29)^2} = 104.7\, MPa$$

Solution 3:
$$M_{max} = \frac{wL^2}{8} = \frac{2 \times 6^2}{8} = 9\,kNm$$

Solution 4:
$$R = \sqrt{5^2 + 5^2} = 7.07\,kN$$

Solution 5:
$V_{base} = -10\,kN$ (Assuming no vertical loads, horizontal load translates directly to a shear force at the base).

Solution 6:
$$P_{cr} = \frac{\pi^2 EI}{(KL)^2}$$
$I = 80 \times 10^{-6}\,m^4;\ E = 200 \times 10^9\,Pa;\ L = 3\,m;\ K = 1$
$$P_{cr} = \frac{\pi^2 \times 200 \times 10^9 \times 80 \times 10^{-6}}{(1 \times 3)^2} = 1.77 \times 10^6\,N$$

Solution 7:
Shear force diagram starts at 5 kN at the left support, drops to -5 kN at the midpoint under the point load, and returns to 0 at the right support.

Solution 8:
$$\tau_{max} = \frac{\sigma_1 - \sigma_2}{2} = \frac{100 - (-50)}{2} = 75\,MPa$$
$$SF = \frac{\tau_y}{\tau_{max}} = \frac{60}{75} = 0.8$$

Solution 9:
$$F_f = \mu_k N = 0.4 \times 200 = 80\,N$$

Solution 10:
$$f = \frac{1}{2\pi}\sqrt{\frac{k}{m}} = \frac{1}{2\pi}\sqrt{\frac{50}{2}} = 1.59\,Hz$$

Chapter 11: Materials

Properties of Materials

Understanding the properties of materials is fundamental in engineering and materials science. It informs material selection, design decisions, and performance assessments across various applications, from aerospace to biomedical engineering. Material properties dictate how substances respond under different conditions, such as mechanical stress, temperature changes, and environmental exposure.

Classification of Material Properties

1. Mechanical Properties:

- **Strength:** The ability of a material to withstand mechanical forces without failure. This includes tensile strength, compressive strength, shear strength, and fatigue strength.
- **Elasticity:** The capacity of a material to return to its original shape after deformation. Quantified by Young's modulus, shear modulus, and bulk modulus.
- **Plasticity:** The degree to which a material can undergo permanent deformation without rupturing.
- **Hardness:** The resistance of a material to permanent indentation or penetration. Measured using tests such as Rockwell, Brinell, and Vickers.
- **Toughness:** The ability to absorb energy before fracturing, combining strength and ductility.
- **Ductility:** The ability to deform under tensile stress; highly ductile materials can be drawn into wire.
- **Brittleness:** The propensity of a material to fracture without significant deformation.

2. Thermal Properties:

- **Thermal Expansion:** The tendency of a material to change in shape, area, and volume in response to a change in temperature.
- **Thermal Conductivity:** The ability of a material to conduct heat.
- **Specific Heat Capacity:** The amount of heat per unit mass required to raise the temperature by one degree Celsius.
- **Thermal Shock Resistance:** The ability of a material to withstand rapid changes in temperature without damage.

3. Electrical Properties:

- **Electrical Conductivity:** The ability of a material to conduct electric current.
- **Resistivity:** The resistance of a material to the flow of electric current.
- **Dielectric Strength:** The maximum electric field that a material can withstand without breaking down.

4. Optical Properties:

- **Refractive Index:** A measure of how much the speed of light is reduced inside a medium.
- **Transparency:** The degree to which a material can transmit light.
- **Luminous Transmittance:** The proportion of visible light that passes through a material.

5. Chemical Properties:

- **Corrosion Resistance:** The ability to withstand damage caused by oxidation or other chemical reactions.
- **Chemical Stability:** A measure of a material's ability to maintain its original chemical structure.

Testing and Measurement of Material Properties

Material properties are typically determined through standardized testing protocols that ensure repeatability and reliability. Common tests include:

- **Tensile Testing:** Determines tensile strength, elasticity, and ductility.
- **Compression Testing:** Measures the behavior of materials under crushing loads.
- **Impact Testing:** Assesses toughness, typically through Charpy or Izod test setups.
- **Hardness Testing:** Determines resistance to indentation and scratching.

Applications and Importance

Understanding material properties allows engineers to:

- **Select appropriate materials** for specific applications based on performance requirements.
- **Predict how materials will behave** under different environmental conditions and loads.
- **Design products** that utilize materials efficiently and safely.
- **Innovate new materials** that meet specialized criteria for advanced applications.

Challenges in Material Properties

1. Variability in Properties: Material properties can vary due to manufacturing conditions, impurities, and processing methods, making it crucial to use precise quality control measures.

2. Environmental and Operational Conditions: Properties can change in response to environmental factors such as humidity, temperature, and exposure to chemicals, requiring robust material selection and design adjustments.

3. Advanced Composite Materials: Composites and high-performance materials may exhibit anisotropic properties, meaning their strength and stiffness vary according to the direction of the load. This adds complexity to design and analysis processes.

Conclusion

The study of material properties is a cornerstone of material science and engineering, crucial for the design and application of all physical products. It bridges the gap between science and application, allowing for the development of innovative solutions across industries. Understanding and manipulating material properties lead to advancements in technology and industrial capabilities, paving the way for future innovations and improved performance standards.

Material Selection:

Material selection is a critical process in engineering and product design, determining the performance, durability, cost, and sustainability of the final product. This decision-making process involves evaluating a material's properties against the operational, environmental, and economic requirements of the application. Effective material selection can optimize functionality, minimize costs, and enhance the overall value of a project.

Principles of Material Selection

1. Performance Requirements: Material selection starts with a clear understanding of the functional requirements of the application. This includes considerations such as mechanical strength, temperature resistance, electrical conductivity, and chemical stability.

2. Economic Considerations: Cost-effectiveness is paramount in material selection. This not only includes the initial cost of the material but also the costs related to processing, fabrication, maintenance, and disposal.

3. Environmental Impact: Sustainability considerations are increasingly important in material selection. Materials should be chosen based on their lifecycle environmental impact, including energy consumption during production, recyclability, and environmental degradation.

Criteria for Material Selection

1. Mechanical Properties: The strength, ductility, hardness, and toughness of a material must align with the mechanical stresses and strains it will encounter in service. Tensile strength, yield strength, and fatigue resistance are typical metrics evaluated.

2. Physical Properties: Thermal properties (like conductivity and expansion), density, and melting point are critical when products must operate under temperature variations or require specific heat management.

3. Chemical Properties: Corrosion resistance and chemical stability are crucial for materials exposed to harsh environments or reactive substances.

4. Manufacturing Compatibility: The selected material must be compatible with intended manufacturing processes such as casting, molding, machining, or welding. This includes considering the material's formability, machinability, and weldability.

5. Aesthetic and Functional Considerations: For consumer products, the aesthetic properties such as color, texture, and finish can be as important as mechanical properties. Additionally, functional considerations like weight, electrical insulation, or transparency may be decisive.

Material Selection Process

1. Define Application Requirements: Detail the operational environment, required lifespan, exposure conditions, and mechanical loads to create a comprehensive profile of what the material needs to withstand.

2. Identify Candidate Materials: Generate a list of potential materials that meet the basic requirements outlined. This can be facilitated by material databases and selection software.

3. Compare and Contrast: Use selection charts and tools to compare materials based on specific selection indices like strength-to-weight ratio, cost-per-performance, or environmental impact metrics.

4. Testing and Prototyping: Physical testing and prototyping may be necessary to validate the choice of material under realistic operating conditions.

5. Lifecycle Considerations: Consider the entire lifecycle of the product, from raw material extraction through manufacturing, use, and disposal, to ensure that the material choice aligns with sustainability goals and compliance with regulations.

Challenges in Material Selection

1. Trade-Offs: Often, selecting a material involves balancing conflicting properties, such as strength versus weight or cost versus performance, requiring a careful evaluation of priorities.

2. Emerging Materials: New materials and composites frequently enter the market, each with limited historical data on performance and long-term reliability.

3. Regulatory and Standards Compliance: Materials must comply with applicable regulations and standards, which may vary by industry and region, complicating the selection process.

Conclusion

Material selection is a multidimensional decision-making process that significantly impacts the engineering and economic success of a project. It requires a thorough understanding of material science, engineering principles, and environmental considerations. By systematically assessing materials against well-defined criteria, engineers can make informed decisions that optimize the performance and sustainability of their projects, ultimately leading to more innovative and successful designs.

Problems:

Problem 1: Properties of Materials Determine the Young's modulus for a material if a force of 10,000 N causes a 5 mm extension in a rod originally 2 meters long with a cross-sectional area of 10 mm².

Problem 2: Material Selection Select the best material for a high-temperature application that requires excellent corrosion resistance and moderate strength.

Problem 3: Mechanical Properties Calculate the tensile strength of a material if it can withstand a maximum load of 500 N before failing, and it has a cross-sectional area of 0.5 cm².

Problem 4: Thermal Properties If a material has a thermal expansion coefficient of 12x10^-6 /°C, calculate the expansion over a length of 1 meter for a temperature increase of 50°C.

Problem 5: Electrical Properties A copper wire has a cross-sectional area of 1 mm² and a length of 10 meters. If the resistivity of copper is 1.68x10^-8 Ωm, calculate the resistance of the wire.

Problem 6: Chemical Properties For a material exposed to a chemical environment, which property would be most critical to consider for material selection?

Problem 7: Physical Properties How does the density of a material affect its selection for aerospace applications?

Problem 8: Manufacturing Compatibility What factor is crucial when selecting a material intended for complex machining operations?

Problem 9: Environmental Impact Assess the importance of recyclability in material selection for consumer electronics.

Problem 10: Lifecycle Considerations Explain why it's important to consider the lifecycle in material selection for a building structure.

Solutions:

Solution 1:

$$E = \frac{Stress}{Strain} = \frac{\frac{F}{A}}{\frac{\Delta L}{L}} = \frac{\frac{10000}{10 \times 10^{-6}}}{\frac{0.005}{2}} = 200\, GPa$$

Solution 2:

Stainless steel or nickel-based alloys are ideal for high-temperature applications requiring corrosion resistance.

Solution 3:

$$Tensile\ Strength = \frac{Maximum\ Load}{Cross-sectional\ Area} = \frac{500}{0.5 \times 10^{-4}} = 1000\ MPa$$

Solution 4:

$$\Delta L = \alpha L \Delta T = 12 \times 10^{-6} \times 1 \times 50 = 0.0006\ meters\ or\ 0.6\ mm$$

Solution 5:

$$R = \rho \frac{L}{A} = 1.68 \times 10^{-8} \times \frac{10}{1 \times 10^{-6}} = 0.168\ \Omega$$

Solution 6:

Corrosion resistance would be the most critical property to consider for a material in a chemical environment.

Solution 7:

Low density is crucial for aerospace applications to reduce overall weight and enhance fuel efficiency.

Solution 8:

Machinability is crucial for materials intended for complex machining operations to ensure the material can be accurately and efficiently shaped.

Solution 9:

Recyclability is essential in consumer electronics to minimize environmental impact and support sustainability efforts.

Solution 10:

Considering the lifecycle in material selection ensures that the building materials are sustainable, cost-effective for maintenance, and suitable for the intended lifespan of the structure.

Chapter 12: Fluid Mechanics

Fluid Properties

Understanding the properties of fluids is fundamental to fluid mechanics, influencing the analysis, design, and operation of systems involving fluid flow, such as pipelines, pumps, and hydraulic systems. Fluid properties affect calculations involving dynamics, statics, and thermal aspects of fluid behavior in both engineering and natural environments.

Key Fluid Properties

1. Density (ρ): Density is a primary characteristic of a fluid, defined as mass per unit volume (kg/m^3) and is a critical factor in buoyancy, pressure, and dynamic calculations. For gases, density can vary significantly with temperature and pressure changes, unlike liquids, which are relatively incompressible.

2. Viscosity (μ): Viscosity is the measure of a fluid's resistance to gradual deformation by shear or tensile stress. It is pivotal in determining the flow behavior:

- **Dynamic Viscosity (μ):** Represented in Pa·s, it describes the internal resistance of a fluid to flow.
- **Kinematic Viscosity (ν):** Given by ν=μ/ρ, expressed in m^2/s, it is used for characterizing flow dynamics without the direct influence of fluid density.

3. Surface Tension (σ): Surface tension results from the cohesive forces between liquid molecules, affecting phenomena such as capillary rise and droplet formation. It is particularly relevant in small-scale applications, such as in microfluidics.

4. Specific Heat Capacity (cp, cv): These properties measure the heat energy required to raise the temperature of a unit mass of a substance by one degree Celsius. cp is the specific heat at constant pressure, and cv is at constant volume, crucial for understanding energy transformations in fluid flow and heat transfer applications.

5. Thermal Conductivity (k): Thermal conductivity is the ability of a fluid to conduct heat, playing a vital role in determining the efficiency of heat exchangers and cooling systems.

6. Vapor Pressure: The pressure at which a liquid boils and turns to vapor at a given temperature. Understanding vapor pressure is essential for applications involving phase change, such as in boilers and condensers.

7. Compressibility: The measure of the change in volume of a fluid under pressure. While liquids are often considered incompressible, gases are highly compressible, impacting calculations in aerodynamics and pneumatics.

Applications and Importance

Fluid properties are integral to:

- **Designing HVAC Systems:** Understanding properties like density, viscosity, and specific heat capacity ensures systems are efficient and effective in temperature control.

- **Hydraulic Systems:** Viscosity affects the efficiency and performance of hydraulic fluids in power transmission.
- **Piping Systems:** Density and viscosity influence the pressure drops and pump requirements.
- **Aerodynamics:** The compressibility of air is crucial for calculations involving high-speed aircraft.

Measurement of Fluid Properties

Accurate measurement of fluid properties is achieved through a variety of instruments and methods:

- **Density is measured using hydrometers or densitometers.**
- **Viscosity can be measured by viscometers, which can be capillary, rotational, or vibrational.**
- **Calorimeters measure specific heat capacity.**
- **Thermal conductivity is often measured using specialized heat flow meters.**

Challenges in Handling Fluid Properties

1. Variable Conditions: Fluid properties can change with environmental conditions like temperature and pressure, complicating the design and operation of systems. **2. Non-Newtonian Fluids:** For fluids that do not follow Newtonian behavior (where viscosity is constant), such as slurries and polymers, specialized models and tests are required. **3. Scaling Effects:** In large systems or those involving rapid changes, dynamic effects can alter the effective behavior of fluid properties, demanding robust control and prediction methodologies.

Conclusion

Fluid properties form the foundation of fluid mechanics, deeply influencing the behavior of fluids in natural and engineered systems. Mastery over these properties allows engineers and scientists to design more efficient, safer, and innovative systems that effectively manage fluid dynamics across various applications, from industrial processes to environmental systems and beyond.

Dynamics:

Fluid dynamics is a critical branch of physics and engineering that deals with the study of fluids (liquids, gases, and plasmas) in motion. It encompasses the analysis of fluid flow behavior, interactions with surrounding environments, and the forces that influence these movements. Understanding fluid dynamics is essential for designing efficient systems in aerospace, marine, automotive, civil engineering, and many other fields.

Fundamental Concepts of Fluid Dynamics

1. Continuity Equation: The continuity equation is based on the principle of conservation of mass in fluid dynamics. For an incompressible fluid, the equation is typically expressed as:

$$\nabla \cdot \mathbf{v} = 0$$

and for compressible flows:

$$\frac{\partial \rho}{\partial t} + \nabla \cdot (\rho \mathbf{v}) = 0$$

where ρ is the fluid density, and $\mathbf{v}$ is the velocity field. This equation ensures that mass is conserved as the fluid flows through different sections of a system.

2. Bernoulli's Equation: Bernoulli's equation is a fundamental relation in fluid dynamics that relates pressure, velocity, and height in a flowing fluid. It is derived from the conservation of energy and is written as:

$$P + \tfrac{1}{2}\rho v^2 + \rho g h = \text{constant}$$

where P is the pressure, ρ is the density of the fluid, v is the velocity of the fluid, g is the acceleration due to gravity, and h is the elevation.

3. Navier-Stokes Equations: The Navier-Stokes equations provide a comprehensive description of fluid motion. These equations account for the forces of viscosity and are used to model virtually all fluid flow scenarios:

$$\rho \left(\frac{\partial \mathbf{v}}{\partial t} + \mathbf{v} \cdot \nabla \mathbf{v} \right) = -\nabla P + \mu \nabla^2 \mathbf{v} + \rho \mathbf{g}$$

where μ is the dynamic viscosity of the fluid.

Applications of Fluid Dynamics

1. Aerospace Engineering: Understanding fluid dynamics is crucial for designing aircraft and spacecraft, focusing on optimizing shapes to reduce drag and enhance lift.

2. Automotive Engineering: Fluid dynamics is used to design more aerodynamic vehicles that offer lower resistance and higher fuel efficiency.

3. Civil Engineering: Hydraulic engineering, a branch of civil engineering, relies on fluid dynamics to design water supply systems, dams, and canals.

4. Environmental Engineering: Fluid dynamics is essential in modeling pollution dispersion, wastewater treatment, and the behavior of natural water bodies.

Measurement and Visualization Techniques

1. Pitot Tubes: Used to measure fluid velocity by converting the kinetic energy of the flow into potential energy.

2. Particle Image Velocimetry (PIV): A sophisticated optical measurement technique that captures the entire velocity fields within fluid flows by tracking the movement of seeded particles illuminated by a laser sheet.

3. Computational Fluid Dynamics (CFD): A numerical analysis tool that uses algorithms and computational methods to solve and analyze problems that involve fluid flows, heavily used for complex simulations where experimental tests might be impractical.

Challenges in Fluid Dynamics

1. Turbulent Flows: Modeling turbulent flows, where chaotic fluid particles move unpredictably, remains one of the most complex aspects of fluid dynamics.

2. Multiphase Flows: Flows involving more than one phase (e.g., liquid-gas, solid-liquid) present significant challenges due to the interaction between different phases.

3. Scale and Realism: Reproducing realistic operational conditions in models and tests can be extremely challenging, particularly for large-scale applications or those involving complex interactions.

Conclusion

Fluid dynamics is a cornerstone of many engineering disciplines, playing a crucial role in the design, analysis, and optimization of systems involving fluid flow. Mastery of this field leads to innovations across a wide range of industries, contributing to advancements in technology, energy conservation, and environmental protection. Understanding fluid behavior not only improves the performance of engineering systems but also enhances our ability to manage natural resources and address environmental challenges.

Flow in Pipes and Open Channels:

Understanding the dynamics of fluid flow within confined conduits like pipes and open channels such as rivers or canals is crucial for civil, environmental, and mechanical engineering. These flow systems are foundational in applications ranging from municipal water supply and wastewater treatment to irrigation and hydraulic engineering.

Fundamentals of Flow in Pipes

1. Types of Flow:

- **Laminar Flow:** Characterized by smooth, parallel layers of fluid, laminar flow occurs at low Reynolds numbers ($typically\ Re < 2000$).

- **Turbulent Flow:** At higher Reynolds numbers ($Re > 4000$), the flow becomes chaotic and mixed. Turbulent flow is more efficient for mixing and mass transfer but increases frictional losses.

- **Transitional Flow:** Occurs between laminar and turbulent flow conditions, where both flow regimes may intermittently appear.

2. Reynolds Number (Re): This dimensionless number is crucial for characterizing the type of flow in a pipe:

$$Re = \frac{\rho v D}{\mu}$$

where ρ is the fluid density, v is the mean velocity, D is the hydraulic diameter, and μ is the dynamic viscosity.

3. Friction Factor and Head Loss: Head loss due to friction is an essential consideration in pipe flow, commonly calculated using the Darcy-Weisbach equation:

$$h_f = f \frac{L}{D} \frac{v^2}{2g}$$

where f is the friction factor, L is the pipe length, g is the acceleration due to gravity, and the other symbols have their usual meanings.

Dynamics of Open Channel Flow

1. Types of Open Channel Flow:

- **Uniform Flow:** Flow depth and velocity remain constant along the channel.
- **Non-uniform Flow:** Flow depth and velocity change along the channel, such as in gradually varied flow (GVF) and rapidly varied flow (RVF).

2. Flow Classification:

- **Subcritical Flow:** Occurs when the flow velocity is less than the wave celerity (slow-moving waves can travel upstream), typically seen in rivers and canals.
- **Supercritical Flow:** Faster than wave celerity, preventing disturbances from traveling upstream, often observed in steep channels.
- **Critical Flow:** Marks the transition point between subcritical and supercritical conditions, where the flow velocity equals the wave celerity.

3. Manning's Equation: For calculating the flow rate in open channels, Manning's equation is widely used:

$$Q = \frac{1}{n} A R^{2/3} S^{1/2}$$

where Q is the flow rate, n is the Manning's roughness coefficient, A is the cross-sectional area, R is the hydraulic radius (area/wetted perimeter), and S is the slope of the energy grade line.

Measurement and Design Considerations

1. Pipe Flow Measurement Techniques:

- **Venturi Meters** and **Orifice Plates:** Used to measure flow rate based on changes in fluid velocity and pressure.
- **Pitot Tubes:** Measure velocity at specific points within the flow.

2. Open Channel Measurement Techniques:

- **Weirs and Flumes:** Structures built across channels to measure flow rate by causing a change in water level.
- **Ultrasonic Flow Meters:** Non-invasive devices that measure flow velocity using the Doppler effect.

Challenges in Managing Fluid Flow

1. Energy Losses: Both pipe and open channel flows are subject to energy losses due to friction, bends, fittings, and changes in flow area, requiring careful design to minimize these losses.

2. Sediment Transport: In open channels, managing sediment transport is crucial to prevent erosion and sedimentation that can alter channel characteristics and reduce flow capacity.

3. Scale and Environmental Impact: Large-scale water transport projects must balance engineering objectives with environmental concerns, such as impacts on aquatic habitats and water quality.

Conclusion

The study of flow in pipes and open channels is integral to fluid mechanics and has wide-ranging applications in many areas of engineering. Understanding these flow characteristics allows engineers to design more efficient, sustainable, and safe water management systems that meet the needs of both society and the environment. Accurate modeling and measurement of these flows are critical to ensuring the optimal performance and reliability of such systems.

Fluid Measurement and Machinery

Fluid measurement and machinery involve the technologies and systems used to measure, control, and manipulate fluid flow in various engineering applications. Accurate fluid measurement is essential for operational efficiency, safety, and compliance in industries such as water treatment, oil and gas, and manufacturing. Similarly, fluid machinery plays a crucial role in systems like pumps, turbines, and compressors, which are integral to the movement and management of fluids in countless engineering processes.

Key Concepts in Fluid Measurement

1. Flow Measurement Techniques:

- **Venturi Meter:** Utilizes a converging section of pipe to increase fluid velocity and a diverging section to decrease it, measuring flow rate through pressure differences.

- **Orifice Plate:** Measures flow rate by constricting the flow with a thin plate that has a precise hole in the center, causing a drop in pressure.

- **Pitot Tube:** Measures fluid velocity using the difference between static and stagnation pressures of the fluid.

- **Rotameter:** A vertical tapered tube containing a freely moving float that rises or falls based on the flow rate.

2. Pressure Measurement:

- **Manometers:** Devices that measure fluid pressure using the height of a fluid column. Common types include U-tube, inverted, and differential manometers.

- **Pressure Transducers:** Convert pressure into an electrical signal, commonly used in digital pressure measurement systems.

3. Level Measurement:

- **Float Gauges:** Measure the height of a fluid in tanks by the position of a float.

- **Ultrasonic Level Sensors:** Use sound waves to determine fluid level by measuring the time delay between sending and receiving the ultrasonic pulse.

Overview of Fluid Machinery

1. Pumps:

- **Centrifugal Pumps:** Use a rotating impeller to add energy to fluids, commonly used for liquids.

- **Positive Displacement Pumps:** Move a fixed amount of fluid with each cycle, effective for viscous liquids and at higher pressures.

2. Turbines:

- **Hydraulic Turbines:** Convert hydraulic energy into mechanical energy, used in hydroelectric power generation.
- **Gas Turbines:** Used in jet engines and power plants, these convert the energy of hot, pressurized gases into mechanical energy.

3. Compressors:

- **Reciprocating Compressors:** Use pistons to compress gases, suitable for high pressures.
- **Rotary Screw Compressors:** Use two meshing helical screws to compress air, favored for continuous operations.

Applications of Fluid Measurement and Machinery

1. Water and Wastewater Management: Fluid machinery is used for pumping, treatment, and distribution of water and wastewater. Measurement systems ensure accurate monitoring and control of flow rates and fluid levels to meet regulatory standards.

2. Process Industries: In industries such as chemical, pharmaceutical, and food processing, precise control of fluid flow, pressure, and level is critical for product quality and process efficiency.

3. Energy Sector: Pumps and turbines are essential in the oil and gas industry for extraction and transportation. In power generation, turbines and compressors play critical roles in both conventional and renewable energy plants.

Challenges in Fluid Measurement and Machinery

1. Accuracy and Calibration: Ensuring the accuracy and regular calibration of measurement devices is crucial to maintain system efficiency and to comply with industry standards.

2. Wear and Maintenance: Fluid machinery requires regular maintenance to address wear and tear, especially in harsh environments or with abrasive or corrosive fluids.

3. Integration and Automation: Integrating fluid measurement and machinery into automated control systems presents challenges in terms of compatibility, data management, and real-time response capabilities.

Conclusion

Fluid measurement and machinery are foundational aspects of fluid mechanics with broad applications across various industries. Mastery of these tools and techniques allows engineers to design more effective, efficient, and reliable systems. Continuous advancements in technology and materials are driving improvements in the precision, durability, and integration of these essential components, pushing the boundaries of what is possible in fluid handling and control.

Problems:

Problem 1: Fluid Properties
Calculate the dynamic viscosity of a fluid with a kinematic viscosity of $1.2 \times 10^{-5}\, m^2/s$ and a density of $850\, kg/m^3$.

Problem 2: Fluid Dynamics
Determine the Reynolds number for water flowing at $1.5\, m/s$ in a pipe with a diameter of $0.1\, m$ and kinematic viscosity $1 \times 10^{-6}\, m^2/s$.

Problem 3: Flow in Pipes
Calculate the head loss in a 50-meter-long pipe with a diameter of 0.05 meters, a flow rate of $0.01\, m^3/s$, and a friction factor of 0.02.

Problem 4: Open Channel Flow
What is the flow rate of water in an open channel with a Manning coefficient of 0.015, a hydraulic radius of $0.3\, m$, and a slope of 0.001?

Problem 5: Flow Measurement
How much is the differential pressure across an orifice plate with a diameter ratio of 0.5 if the upstream velocity is $2\, m/s$?

Problem 6: Centrifugal Pump Performance
A centrifugal pump delivers $0.02\, m^3/s$ at a total head of $20\, m$. Calculate the power required by the pump assuming 70% efficiency.

Problem 7: Fluid Dynamics
If the gauge pressure at the bottom of a tank containing oil ($\rho = 900\, kg/m^3$) is $150\, kPa$, find the depth of the oil in the tank.

Problem 8: Turbine Efficiency
Calculate the theoretical power output for a turbine with an efficiency of 80% if $0.1\, m^3/s$ of water drops through a height of $50\, m$.

Problem 9: Viscosity Measurement
Determine the dynamic viscosity if a viscometer measures a shear stress of $0.5\, Pa$ at a shear rate of $400\, s^{-1}$.

Problem 10: Hydraulic Radius

Find the hydraulic radius for a rectangular channel that is $2\,m$ wide and $1.5\,m$ deep, filled to a depth of $1\,m$.

Solutions:

Solution 1:
$$\mu = \nu\rho = 1.2 \times 10^{-5} \times 850 = 0.0102\,\text{Pa}\cdot\text{s}$$

Solution 2:
$$Re = \frac{vD}{\nu} = \frac{1.5 \times 0.1}{1 \times 10^{-6}} = 150{,}000$$

Solution 3:
$$h_f = f\frac{L}{D}\frac{v^2}{2g}$$
$$v = \frac{Q}{A} = \frac{0.01}{\frac{\pi \times (0.05)^2}{4}} = 5.093\,m/s$$
$$h_f = 0.02 \times \frac{50}{0.05} \times \frac{5.093^2}{2 \times 9.81} = 26.13\,m$$

Solution 4:
$$Q = \frac{1}{n}AR^{2/3}S^{1/2} = \frac{1}{0.015} \times (0.3 \times \text{wetted perimeter}) \times 0.3^{2/3} \times 0.001^{1/2}$$
(Assume an appropriate wetted perimeter or additional information as needed.)

Solution 5:
$$\Delta P = \tfrac{1}{2}\rho(v_2^2 - v_1^2)$$
Using continuity and Bernoulli's equations, calculate v_2 from the given diameters and velocities.

Solution 6:
$$P = \frac{\rho g Q H}{\eta} = \frac{1000 \times 9.81 \times 0.02 \times 20}{0.70} = 5.6\,kW$$

Solution 7:
$$h = \frac{P}{\rho g} = \frac{150000}{900 \times 9.81} = 17.02\,m$$

Solution 8:
$$P = \eta\rho g Q H = 0.80 \times 1000 \times 9.81 \times 0.1 \times 50 = 39.24\,kW$$

Solution 9:
$$\mu = \frac{\tau}{\dot{\gamma}} = \frac{0.5}{400} = 0.00125 \, \text{Pa} \cdot \text{s}$$

Solution 10:
$$R = \frac{A}{P} = \frac{2 \times 1}{2+1+2} = 0.2 \, m$$

Chapter 13: Basic Electrical Engineering

Electrical Fundamentals

Electrical fundamentals form the cornerstone of electrical engineering, encompassing the essential principles and theories that govern the behavior of electrical circuits, devices, and systems. Understanding these basics is crucial for designing, analyzing, and troubleshooting electrical equipment and infrastructure.

Key Concepts in Electrical Fundamentals

1. Charge and Current:

- **Electric Charge:** A fundamental property of matter carried by subatomic particles, electric charge is quantified in coulombs (C). Charges are of two types: positive and negative.

- **Electric Current:** The rate of flow of electric charge through a conductor or circuit, measured in amperes (A). Current can flow in two forms:
    - **Direct Current (DC):** Flows in a constant direction, typical in battery-powered devices.
    - **Alternating Current (AC):** Changes direction periodically, commonly used in power systems due to efficient transmission over long distances.

2. Voltage:

- **Voltage (or Electric Potential Difference):** The work needed per unit charge to move a charge between two points in a circuit. Voltage is measured in volts (V) and is the driving force behind the flow of current through a circuit.

3. Resistance and Conductance:

- **Resistance:** A material's opposition to the flow of electric current, measured in ohms (Ω). It depends on the material, cross-sectional area, and length of the conductor.

- **Conductance:** The reciprocal of resistance, measured in siemens (S), representing how easily a material allows the flow of electric current.

4. Power:

- **Electric Power:** The rate at which electrical energy is transferred by an electric circuit, measured in watts (W). Power can be calculated using the formula:

$$P = VI$$

where V is voltage and I is current. In resistive circuits, it can also be expressed as:

$$P = I^2 R$$
$$P = \frac{V^2}{R}$$

5. Energy:

- **Electrical Energy:** The capacity to do work through electric potential, measured in joules (J). It is the product of power and time, commonly billed in kilowatt-hours (kWh) for domestic and industrial electricity use.

Foundations of Circuit Theory

1. Ohm's Law: A fundamental principle stating that the current through a conductor between two points is directly proportional to the voltage across the two points and inversely proportional to the resistance between them:

$$V = IR$$

2. Kirchhoff's Laws:

- **Kirchhoff's Current Law (KCL):** The total current entering a junction must equal the total current leaving the junction.
- **Kirchhoff's Voltage Law (KVL):** The total sum of electrical potential differences around any closed network is zero.

Applications of Electrical Fundamentals

Understanding these basic principles enables the design and functioning of:

- **Electronic Devices:** Utilizing principles like Ohm's Law and the behavior of currents and voltages to function correctly.
- **Electrical Systems:** Designing systems for power generation, transmission, and distribution based on electrical laws.
- **Control Systems:** Managing the operation of motors, generators, and transformers within specified safe and efficient parameters.

Challenges in Electrical Fundamentals

1. Material Limitations: Properties like resistance change with temperature and wear, affecting the performance of electrical systems.

2. System Complexity: As systems increase in complexity, maintaining stability and efficiency while adhering to fundamental electrical laws becomes challenging.

3. Energy Efficiency: Designing systems that minimize energy loss and increase efficiency is crucial in the face of growing environmental concerns and rising energy costs.

Conclusion

Electrical fundamentals are essential for any aspiring engineer, providing the tools necessary to navigate and innovate within the field of electrical engineering. Mastery of these basics not only aids in effective design and analysis but also ensures the reliability and safety of electrical devices and systems across various applications.

Circuit Laws and Analysis

Circuit laws and analysis provide the foundational principles necessary for understanding and predicting the behavior of electrical circuits. These laws are crucial for designing and troubleshooting circuits in both theoretical and practical applications across various fields in electrical engineering.

Key Principles in Circuit Analysis

1. Ohm's Law: Ohm's Law is the fundamental building block of circuit analysis, stating that the current through a conductor between two points is directly proportional to the voltage across the two points and inversely proportional to the resistance:

$$V = IR$$

where V is the voltage, I is the current, and R is the resistance. This law is applicable to both AC and DC circuits.

2. Kirchhoff's Laws:

- **Kirchhoff's Current Law (KCL):** This law states that the total current entering a junction (or node) equals the total current leaving the junction. It is based on the principle of conservation of electric charge.

$$\sum I_{in} = \sum I_{out}$$

- **Kirchhoff's Voltage Law (KVL):** According to this law, the sum of the electrical potential differences (voltage) around any closed network or loop is zero. It is derived from the conservation of energy.

$$\sum V = 0$$

Techniques in Circuit Analysis

1. Node-Voltage Analysis (Node Analysis): This method involves choosing nodes in a circuit and applying KCL to find the voltages at each node relative to a reference node (ground). It is particularly useful in circuits with several components connected between nodes.

2. Mesh Current Analysis (Loop Analysis): Mesh analysis involves writing KVL equations for independent loops in a circuit. The goal is to find the mesh currents, which helps determine the current through each component in those loops.

3. Thevenin's and Norton's Theorems:

- **Thevenin's Theorem:** Simplifies a linear circuit with multiple voltages and resistances to a single voltage source and series resistance when viewed from two terminals.

- **Norton's Theorem:** Similar to Thevenin's theorem but simplifies the circuit to a single current source in parallel with a single resistance.

4. Superposition Theorem: The superposition theorem states that in a linear circuit with multiple sources, the voltage or current at any component is the algebraic sum of the voltages or currents caused by each source acting independently while other sources are replaced by their internal impedances.

Applications of Circuit Laws and Analysis

- **Electrical Networks:** Designing and analyzing networks like power distribution systems for homes or industries.

- **Consumer Electronics:** Developing and testing consumer electronic devices, ensuring functionality and safety.

- **Signal Processing:** Applied in designing circuits for audio and video processing, where signal integrity is paramount.

Challenges in Circuit Analysis

1. Non-linear Components: Components like diodes and transistors do not follow Ohm's Law, requiring more complex analysis methods like piecewise linearization. **2. Real-World Conditions:** Factors like temperature variations, electromagnetic interference, and aging can affect component characteristics, complicating predictions from theoretical analysis. **3. High-Frequency Circuits:** At high frequencies, parasitic elements (capacitance and inductance) become significant, altering the behavior predicted by simple circuit models.

Conclusion

Circuit laws and analysis are critical tools in the toolbox of any electrical engineer, enabling the design and maintenance of stable and efficient electrical systems. Mastery of these concepts allows engineers to innovate and adapt to the evolving technological landscape, ensuring robust and efficient electrical designs.

AC and DC Circuits

Alternating Current (AC) and Direct Current (DC) circuits form the backbone of electrical and electronics engineering, each with unique characteristics and applications. Understanding the differences and operational principles of AC and DC circuits is crucial for designing, implementing, and maintaining a wide range of electrical systems, from residential wiring to sophisticated electronic devices.

Fundamentals of DC Circuits

1. Characteristics: DC circuits involve electricity flowing in one direction, originating from sources such as batteries or DC generators. The voltage in a DC circuit is constant, making these circuits simpler and more predictable than their AC counterparts.

2. Basic Components:

- **Resistors:** Implement resistance to the flow of current, used for controlling current and voltage levels.

- **Capacitors:** Store energy in an electric field, used in filtering applications to smooth varying DC signals.

- **Inductors:** Store energy in a magnetic field, typically used to manage spikes in current.

3. Analysis Techniques: DC circuit analysis often involves applying Ohm's Law and Kirchhoff's Circuit Laws (KCL and KVL) to calculate voltages, currents, and resistances. Thevenin's and Norton's theorems are also widely used for simplifying complex circuits into single-source networks.

Fundamentals of AC Circuits

1. Characteristics: AC circuits feature electricity that alternates its direction and changes its magnitude continuously in a sinusoidal manner. Common in household and industrial power systems, AC can be easily transformed to different voltages, significantly enhancing its utility over long distances.

2. Basic Components:

- **Resistors:** Behave similarly as in DC circuits, impeding current by dissipating energy as heat.
- **Capacitors and Inductors:** Their reactive properties become prominent in AC circuits. Capacitors oppose changes in voltage, while inductors oppose changes in current, both creating phase differences between current and voltage.
- **Transformers:** Used to increase or decrease AC voltages efficiently over long distances.

3. Analysis Techniques: AC circuit analysis requires more complex techniques like phasor diagrams and complex impedance methods. These techniques account for the phase differences between current and voltage introduced by capacitors and inductors.

Comparing AC and DC Circuits

1. Power Generation and Transmission: While DC was initially the standard for early electrical power systems, AC has become the predominant form due to its ease of voltage transformation and lower transmission losses over long distances. However, advancements in technology have seen a resurgence in high-voltage DC (HVDC) systems for specific applications where they outperform AC systems.

2. Applications:

- **DC Applications:** Ideal for low-voltage or battery-powered devices such as mobile phones, laptops, and other personal electronics.
- **AC Applications:** More suited for powering homes, offices, and industries where appliances require larger amounts of power.

3. Safety Considerations: DC is generally safer to handle at lower voltages, whereas AC can be more hazardous due to its alternating nature, which can disrupt the human heartbeat more readily at high voltages.

Challenges in AC and DC Circuits

1. Conversion and Compatibility: Devices that use different types of currents often require converters. For example, electronic devices typically operate on DC and must convert AC from power outlets using adapters.

2. Efficiency Issues: While AC is more efficient for transmitting power over distances, DC is more efficient in energy storage and is increasingly used in renewable energy systems where energy from solar panels or batteries is inherently DC.

3. Complex Designs: AC circuits can become complex, especially in industrial applications where phase synchronization and power factor correction are critical.

Conclusion

AC and DC circuits each have their distinct advantages and are fundamental to modern electrical engineering and technology. Understanding both types of circuits allows engineers to optimize electrical systems for a wide range of applications, ensuring efficiency, safety, and reliability. As technologies evolve, the integration of both AC and DC systems continues to be a critical area of development in electrical infrastructure and device design.

Electrical Measurement Devices

Electrical measurement devices are essential tools in the field of electrical engineering, designed to quantify and analyze various electrical parameters such as voltage, current, resistance, and power. These devices not only help in troubleshooting and maintaining systems but also in designing and testing new electrical equipment.

Types of Electrical Measurement Devices

1. Multimeters:

- **Functionality:** Multimeters are versatile instruments that can measure voltage, current, and resistance. They are available in digital and analog formats, with digital multimeters (DMMs) providing more accuracy and reliability.

- **Applications:** Used for basic troubleshooting, service, and field test applications. Ideal for checking continuity, testing batteries, and performing household electrical inspections.

2. Oscilloscopes:

- **Functionality:** Oscilloscopes display the waveform of electrical signals, showing how signals change over time. They allow measurement of the waveform's amplitude, frequency, rise time, time interval, distortion, and others.

- **Applications:** Critical in the development and testing of electronic devices where dynamic signal behavior needs analysis, such as in telecommunications, automotive, and consumer electronics industries.

3. Clamp Meters:

- **Functionality:** Clamp meters measure the current flowing through a conductor without needing to make direct contact with the circuit. This is achieved by clamping the device around the conductor.

- **Applications:** Widely used by electricians for routine maintenance and checking systems without interrupting the circuit. Ideal for high-current measurements in industrial applications.

4. Voltmeters and Ammeters:

- **Functionality:** Voltmeters measure the electrical potential difference between two points in an electric circuit, while ammeters measure electrical current.

- **Applications:** Voltmeters are used in virtually every sector that deals with electrical systems. Ammeters are crucial in applications where precise current measurements are required, such as in power distribution and electrical testing.

5. Wattmeters:

- **Functionality:** Wattmeters are used to measure the power in an electrical circuit. They can be analog or digital and are capable of measuring both AC and DC power.
- **Applications:** Essential in power management studies, energy audits, and for monitoring power usage in industrial and residential applications.

6. Megohmmeters (Insulation Testers):

- **Functionality:** Megohmmeters apply high voltage to insulation materials to determine the insulation resistance.
- **Applications:** Used to ensure that electrical insulation in wires, motor windings, and cables meets safety standards.

7. Network Analyzers:

- **Functionality:** Network analyzers are used to measure network parameters in electrical networks, such as impedance, reflection, transmission, and S-parameters.
- **Applications:** Crucial in the design and testing of radio frequency (RF) and high-frequency circuitry, providing detailed insights into network behavior.

Challenges in Using Electrical Measurement Devices

1. Accuracy and Calibration: Accuracy is a pivotal concern, especially in precision engineering applications. Regular calibration is necessary to ensure that devices provide accurate measurements over time.

2. Electromagnetic Interference (EMI): EMI can affect the precision of sensitive measurement devices. Proper shielding, grounding, and use of differential measurement techniques are required to mitigate these effects.

3. High Voltage and Current Measurements: Measuring high voltages and currents can pose safety risks and technical challenges. Devices designed for high voltage and current measurements often require special components and insulation to handle extreme values safely.

Conclusion

Electrical measurement devices are indispensable in the electrical engineering landscape, facilitating the development, testing, maintenance, and repair of electrical systems. Advances in technology continue to enhance the functionality, accuracy, and safety of these devices, expanding their applications and effectiveness. Understanding and effectively utilizing these tools is essential for any electrical engineer aiming to maintain system performance and ensure operational safety in a rapidly evolving technological environment.

Three-Phase Systems

Three-phase electrical systems are a fundamental method of alternating current electric power generation, transmission, and distribution. They are used to power large motors and other heavy loads because they efficiently handle high power while maintaining a constant power flow. Understanding three-phase systems is crucial for engineers working in industries ranging from utilities to manufacturing.

Fundamentals of Three-Phase Systems

1. Basic Principles:

- **Phases:** A three-phase system consists of three different AC electrical currents, each with the same frequency and amplitude, operating in a synchronized manner but with each phase offset by one-third of a period (120 degrees).

- **Efficiency:** This configuration allows for a more efficient power distribution system by balancing the loads and reducing conductor material compared to single-phase systems.

2. Configuration Types:

- **Star (Y) Connection:** In a star-connected system, one end of each phase winding is connected to form a common neutral point. The voltage across each phase is root three times less than the line voltage.

- **Delta (Δ) Connection:** In a delta configuration, the end of each phase winding is connected to the beginning of another, forming a closed loop. The line voltage is equal to the phase voltage in this setup.

3. Power in Three-Phase Systems: The total power in a three-phase system is the sum of the power in each phase. The expression for total power is:

$$P = \sqrt{3} \times V_L \times I_L \times \cos(\phi)$$

where V_L is the line voltage, I_L is the line current, and ϕ is the phase angle between the current and voltage.

Applications of Three-Phase Systems

- **Industrial Applications:** Most industrial facilities use three-phase systems to power motors, drives, and other heavy machinery, given their ability to provide continuous power transfer.

- **Commercial Buildings:** Larger commercial buildings typically use three-phase power for HVAC systems, lighting, and elevators due to its load balance and efficiency.

- **Power Grids:** Electrical utilities distribute power in three-phase systems because they optimize the transfer of electrical power over long distances.

Advantages of Three-Phase Systems

- **Continuous Power Delivery:** Unlike single-phase power, which has pulsations, three-phase power has a constant power delivery throughout the cycle, which is crucial for the smooth operation of large motors and equipment.

- **Reduced Conductor Material:** Three-phase systems require less conductor material to transmit electrical power of the same voltage and power capacity compared to single-phase or two-phase systems.

- **Improved Motor Performance:** Motors running on three-phase power exhibit smoother operation, greater efficiency, and a longer lifespan compared to those operating on single-phase power.

Measurement and Safety in Three-Phase Systems

- **Measurement Tools:** Devices such as three-phase power meters and clamp meters are essential for measuring the current and voltage in each phase to ensure balanced loads and to troubleshoot issues.

- **Safety Considerations:** Working with three-phase power involves higher voltages and currents, necessitating stringent safety protocols to prevent electrical accidents, including proper grounding, insulation, and the use of protective gear.

Challenges in Three-Phase Systems

- **Complexity in Installation and Maintenance:** The wiring and maintenance of three-phase systems are more complex compared to single-phase systems, requiring skilled technicians and engineers.

- **Load Balancing:** Uneven loading of phases can lead to system inefficiency and increased wear on equipment, which makes regular monitoring and adjustment essential.

- **Cost:** Although more efficient, the initial setup cost for three-phase systems is higher than that for single-phase systems due to more complex infrastructure requirements.

Conclusion

Three-phase systems represent a critical infrastructure component in modern electrical engineering, offering advantages in terms of efficiency, power delivery, and system stability. Mastery of three-phase system design, operation, and safety is essential for electrical engineers tasked with managing the electrical needs of large-scale industrial, commercial, and utility operations. Understanding these systems enables engineers to optimize electrical systems for performance, safety, and economic viability.

Problems:

Problem 1: Electrical Fundamentals Calculate the current flowing through a resistor of 5 ohms if the voltage across it is 10 volts.

Problem 2: Circuit Laws and Analysis Determine the total resistance in a circuit if three resistors of 2 ohms, 3 ohms, and 6 ohms are connected in series.

Problem 3: AC and DC Circuits What is the impedance of a circuit containing a 4 ohm resistor and a 3 ohm inductive reactance in series?

Problem 4: Electrical Measurement Devices A voltmeter with a range of 0-300V is connected across a resistor. If the voltmeter reads 120 volts, what is the power dissipated by the resistor if the current is 2 amps?

Problem 5: Three-Phase Systems Calculate the line current in a balanced three-phase system where each phase has an impedance of 8+j68 + j68+j6 ohms and the line-to-line voltage is 240 volts.

Problem 6: Electrical Fundamentals What is the power factor of a circuit with an apparent power of 100 VA and a real power of 80 W?

Problem 7: Circuit Laws and Analysis Using Kirchhoff's Voltage Law, calculate the voltage drop across a 10 ohm resistor if it is part of a loop with a 9V battery and another resistor of 5 ohms, assuming a current of 0.5 A flows through the loop.

Problem 8: AC and DC Circuits An AC circuit has a capacitive reactance of 5 ohms and is powered by a 50 Hz source. Calculate the capacitance.

Problem 9: Electrical Measurement Devices How would you measure the power consumption of an appliance using a wattmeter?

Problem 10: Three-Phase Systems In a delta-connected three-phase system, if the phase voltage is 120V, what is the line voltage?

Solutions:

Solution 1:
$$I = \frac{V}{R} = \frac{10}{5} = 2 \text{ amps}$$

Solution 2:
$$R_{total} = R_1 + R_2 + R_3 = 2 + 3 + 6 = 11 \text{ ohms}$$

Solution 3:
$$Z = R + jX_L = 4 + j3 \text{ ohms}$$

Solution 4:
$$P = VI = 120 \times 2 = 240 \text{ W}$$

Solution 5:

For balanced three-phase $V_{phase} = \frac{V_{line}}{\sqrt{3}} = \frac{240}{\sqrt{3}} \approx 138.6$ volts

$I_{line} = \frac{V_{phase}}{Z} = \frac{138.6}{10} = 13.86$ amps

(NB: Magnitude of Z calculated as $Z = \sqrt{R^2 + X^2} = \sqrt{8^2 + 6^2} = 10$ ohms)

Solution 6:

Power Factor $= \frac{P}{S} = \frac{80}{100} = 0.8$

Solution 7:

$V = IR = 0.5 \times 10 = 5$ volts

Solution 8:

$X_C = \frac{1}{2\pi f C}$

$C = \frac{1}{2\pi f X_C} = \frac{1}{2\pi \times 50 \times 5} = 0.000636$ farads

Solution 9:

Connect the wattmeter in series with the appliance, ensuring the current coil is in series with the circuit and the voltage coil is across the appliance. Measure the real power directly from the wattmeter reading.

Solution 10:

$V_{line} = V_{phase} \times \sqrt{3} = 120 \times \sqrt{3} \approx 208$ volts

Chapter 14: Thermodynamics and Heat Transfer

Thermodynamic Laws and Equilibrium

Thermodynamics is a fundamental branch of physics and engineering that deals with the relationships between heat, work, temperature, and energy. The laws of thermodynamics govern how these quantities interact in various systems, and understanding these laws is crucial for analyzing and designing engines, refrigerators, and even complex chemical reactions. Thermodynamic equilibrium is a state where certain properties of the system do not change unless disturbed by external actions.

The Laws of Thermodynamics

1. Zeroth Law of Thermodynamics: The Zeroth Law establishes the concept of temperature and thermal equilibrium. It states that if two systems are each in thermal equilibrium with a third system, they are also in thermal equilibrium with each other. This law forms the basis for temperature measurement and indicates that temperature is a fundamental and measurable property of matter.

2. First Law of Thermodynamics (Law of Energy Conservation): The First Law states that the total energy of an isolated system is constant; energy can be transformed from one form to another but cannot be created or destroyed. In mathematical terms, it is expressed as:

$$\Delta U = Q - W$$

where ΔU is the change in internal energy of the system, Q is the heat added to the system, and W is the work done by the system on its surroundings. This law is essentially a statement of the conservation of energy principle, adapted for thermodynamic systems.

3. Second Law of Thermodynamics: This law introduces the concept of entropy, a measure of system disorder or randomness. The Second Law states that the total entropy of an isolated system can never decrease over time. It also establishes that heat cannot spontaneously transfer from a colder to a hotter body. As a result, it sets the direction of heat transfer and the possible efficiency of heat engines. The law can be expressed in several ways, but one common form is:

$$\Delta S \geq \frac{Q}{T}$$

for any spontaneous process, where ΔS is the change in entropy, Q is the heat transfer, and T is the absolute temperature.

4. Third Law of Thermodynamics: The Third Law states that as the temperature of a system approaches absolute zero, the entropy of the system approaches a constant minimum. This law has implications for reaching absolute zero temperature in practice, suggesting that it is unattainable because doing so would require an infinite number of steps.

Thermodynamic Equilibrium

In thermodynamic equilibrium, a system's macroscopic properties such as pressure, temperature, and volume remain constant over time. Equilibrium can be categorized into different types depending on which properties remain constant:

- **Thermal Equilibrium:** No temperature gradient exists within the system, thus no heat transfer occurs.
- **Mechanical Equilibrium:** There are no changes in pressure at any part of the system, and no mechanical work is done.
- **Chemical Equilibrium:** The chemical composition of the system does not change over time, indicating that the rates of forward and reverse chemical reactions are equal.

Applications of Thermodynamic Laws and Equilibrium

The laws of thermodynamics and the concept of equilibrium have wide-ranging applications:

- **Energy Production:** Power plants and engines are designed based on these principles to maximize efficiency.
- **Environmental Systems:** The behavior of the atmosphere and oceans is governed by thermodynamic principles.
- **Material Science:** Understanding phase changes and material properties under different conditions.
- **Chemical Industry:** Design of chemical reactors and processes relies heavily on thermodynamic equilibrium.

Challenges and Considerations

The complexity of real systems often requires simplifications and assumptions to apply thermodynamic laws effectively. Dealing with non-equilibrium states, where the laws are not directly applicable, requires advanced techniques and understanding. Moreover, accurately measuring system properties such as temperature and pressure is crucial but can be challenging in extreme conditions.

Conclusion

Thermodynamic laws and the concept of thermodynamic equilibrium form the bedrock upon which much of classical and modern physics and engineering rest. Mastery of these concepts is essential for engineers and scientists who deal with energy transformations in any form, ensuring the development of systems that are both efficient and sustainable in long-term applications.

Thermodynamic Properties and Processes

Thermodynamic properties are key characteristics that define the state of a thermodynamic system, and understanding these properties is crucial for analyzing and designing systems involving energy transfer and transformation. Thermodynamic processes, on the other hand, describe the pathway taken by a system as it moves from one state to another, often involving changes in properties like temperature, pressure, volume, and entropy.

Fundamental Thermodynamic Properties

1. Temperature and Pressure:

- **Temperature** is a measure of the average kinetic energy of the particles in a substance. It is fundamental to the phase behavior of substances and their thermal energy content.
- **Pressure** is the force exerted per unit area by the molecules of a fluid. It is a critical factor in determining the state and phase of materials under different conditions.

2. Volume and Specific Volume:

- **Volume** is the space occupied by a substance, and understanding its variation with temperature and pressure is essential for processes like compression and expansion.
- **Specific Volume** is the volume per unit mass of a substance, commonly used in calculations involving gases.

3. Internal Energy:

- **Internal Energy** represents the total energy stored within a system, comprising kinetic and potential energies of molecules. It is a state function and is crucial in analyzing energy changes in a system without involving the kinetic or potential energy of the system as a whole.

4. Enthalpy:

- **Enthalpy** is a measure of the total heat content of a system and is used extensively in processes where heat transfer occurs at constant pressure, such as in boilers and condensers.

5. Entropy:

- **Entropy** measures the disorder or randomness of a system and is a key concept in determining the direction of spontaneous processes and the efficiency of energy conversion systems.

6. Gibbs Free Energy:

- **Gibbs Free Energy** is the useful work obtainable from a system at constant temperature and pressure. It is fundamental in chemical reaction thermodynamics, predicting the spontaneity of reactions and phase transitions.

Key Thermodynamic Processes

1. Isothermal Process:

- An **isothermal process** occurs at a constant temperature, implying that the internal energy change for an ideal gas is zero, and any heat added to the system is used to do work.

2. Adiabatic Process:

- In an **adiabatic process**, no heat is transferred into or out of the system, meaning that any change in internal energy of the system is directly related to the work done by or on the system.

3. Isobaric Process:

- An **isobaric process** takes place at a constant pressure. The heat transferred to the system changes its internal energy and can also perform work by changing the volume of the system.

4. Isochoric Process:

- An **isochoric process**, also known as an isovolumetric process, occurs at a constant volume. Here, no work is done, and any heat added changes the internal energy of the system.

Applications of Thermodynamic Properties and Processes

- **Energy Systems:** Understanding these properties and processes is essential for designing systems that convert thermal energy into mechanical work, such as in steam turbines and internal combustion engines.

- **Refrigeration and Air Conditioning:** The principles of thermodynamics guide the design of systems that transfer heat to achieve desired temperatures and humidity levels.

- **Material Science:** Thermodynamic properties are crucial in studying material behaviors under various thermal conditions, influencing new material designs and manufacturing processes.

Challenges in Practical Applications

- **Measurement Accuracy:** Accurately measuring thermodynamic properties, especially under extreme conditions, is challenging and requires sophisticated equipment.

- **System Irreversibilities:** Real systems often involve irreversibilities (like friction and turbulence), making theoretical models less accurate without adjustments.

- **Environmental and Economic Constraints:** Designing thermodynamic processes that are both environmentally friendly and economically viable is increasingly challenging, requiring innovative approaches and technologies.

Conclusion

Thermodynamic properties and processes form the foundation of much of engineering practice, particularly in fields involving heat and energy transfer. Mastery of these concepts enables engineers to design more efficient, effective, and sustainable systems across a wide range of applications, from industrial manufacturing to environmental management. Understanding and manipulating these properties and processes ensure that engineers can develop solutions that meet the needs of today's technology-driven society.

Heat Transfer Methods

Heat transfer is a fundamental phenomenon in thermodynamics that involves the movement of thermal energy from one body or substance to another. This process is crucial in numerous applications, including HVAC systems, industrial manufacturing, automotive engineering, and energy systems. Understanding the methods of heat transfer—conduction, convection, and radiation—is essential for designing efficient and effective thermal management systems.

Conduction

1. Basics of Conduction: Conduction is the process by which heat is transferred through a material without any movement of the material itself. It occurs due to the temperature gradient within the material, where molecules at a higher temperature transfer their energy to adjacent lower-temperature molecules.

2. Governing Law: The rate of heat transfer by conduction is governed by Fourier's Law:

$$q = -k\nabla T$$

where q is the heat flux, k is the thermal conductivity of the material, and ∇T is the temperature gradient. The negative sign indicates that heat flows from higher to lower temperatures.

3. Applications: Conduction is critical in applications involving solid materials, such as building insulation, heat sinks in electronics, and thermal barriers in engines.

Convection

1. Basics of Convection: Convection involves the transfer of heat by the physical movement of a fluid (liquid or gas). This process can be natural (due to buoyancy forces caused by temperature differences within the fluid) or forced (by external means such as a fan or pump).

2. Governing Equations: The rate of heat transfer by convection can be expressed using Newton's Law of Cooling:

$$q = hA(T_s - T_\infty)$$

where h is the convective heat transfer coefficient, A is the surface area, T_s is the surface temperature, and T_∞ is the fluid temperature far from the surface.

3. Applications: Convection is used in a wide range of applications, including HVAC systems, cooling of electronic components, automotive radiators, and food processing.

Radiation

1. Basics of Radiation: Radiation is the transfer of heat through electromagnetic waves without requiring a medium. All bodies emit thermal radiation depending on their temperature.

2. Governing Law: The Stefan-Boltzmann Law quantifies the power radiated from a black body in terms of its temperature:

$$E = \sigma T^4$$

where E is the emissive power, σ is the Stefan-Boltzmann constant, and T is the absolute temperature of the body.

3. Applications: Radiation is a key heat transfer method in space applications (where convection is impossible), solar energy systems, and high-temperature industrial processes.

Combined Heat Transfer Modes

In many practical applications, these three modes of heat transfer work in conjunction to affect the overall heat transfer system. For instance:

- In a boiling kettle, heat from the stove is conducted through the metal base, convective currents distribute the heat through the water, and heat is lost through radiation and convection from the water surface to the surrounding air.

- In thermal management of electronic devices, conduction moves heat away from components to a heat sink, where convection (often enhanced by a fan) dissipates the heat into the ambient air.

Challenges in Heat Transfer

1. Optimizing Heat Transfer Coefficients: Designing systems that maximize or minimize heat transfer efficiently, depending on the application, can be challenging due to material limitations and system geometry.

2. Managing Thermal Stresses: Thermal stresses caused by heat transfer can lead to material fatigue and failure, especially in systems experiencing wide temperature gradients.

3. Environmental and Economic Considerations: Heat transfer systems must often be designed with considerations of energy efficiency and environmental impact, balancing performance with sustainability.

Conclusion

The study of heat transfer methods forms an essential part of thermodynamics, with broad applications across various fields of engineering. An in-depth understanding of conduction, convection, and radiation, along with their practical implications, enables engineers to design more innovative, efficient, and effective systems tailored to specific operational needs. This knowledge not only aids in optimizing thermal management solutions but also contributes significantly to advances in energy conservation and sustainability.

Psychrometrics

Psychrometrics is the study of the thermodynamic properties of moist air and its interactions with physical materials, particularly water vapor. It is a critical field in HVAC (heating, ventilation, and air conditioning) engineering, meteorology, and industries requiring precise control of humidity and temperature.

Fundamental Concepts in Psychrometrics

1. Psychrometric Chart: The psychrometric chart is a visual representation of the physical and thermal properties of air-water vapor mixtures at a constant pressure. It includes properties such as dry bulb temperature, wet bulb temperature, dew point, relative humidity, specific humidity, and enthalpy.

2. Dry Bulb Temperature (DBT): This is the temperature of air measured by a standard thermometer exposed to the air stream. It does not consider the moisture content of the air.

3. Wet Bulb Temperature (WBT): Measured using a thermometer with the bulb wrapped in wet muslin over which air passes, the wet bulb temperature is a key indicator of the air's moisture content. It is crucial for calculating the air's capacity to hold moisture and for assessing evaporation cooling potential.

4. Dew Point Temperature: The temperature at which air becomes saturated with moisture and dew begins to form. The dew point is a direct indicator of the moisture content in the air; higher dew points indicate higher moisture levels.

5. Relative Humidity (RH): Expressed as a percentage, relative humidity is the ratio of the current absolute humidity to the highest possible absolute humidity at that temperature. RH is a critical factor in human comfort, building design, and the storage of sensitive materials.

6. Specific Humidity and Absolute Humidity: Specific humidity is the mass of water vapor per unit mass of dry air, while absolute humidity is the mass of water vapor per unit volume of air. Both are vital for processes involving drying, cooling, and controlling air quality.

Psychrometric Processes

1. Heating and Cooling:

- **Heating:** Involves increasing the DBT of the air, often without changing its moisture content significantly.
- **Cooling:** Reduces the DBT, and can also decrease the air's moisture content as it approaches the dew point, causing condensation.

2. Humidification and Dehumidification:

- **Humidification:** Adding moisture to the air, which is essential in dry climates for comfort and to maintain material properties.
- **Dehumidification:** Removing moisture from the air, crucial in humid climates to prevent mold growth and to maintain comfort levels.

3. Adiabatic Mixing of Two Air Streams: Common in HVAC systems where two air streams of different thermodynamic properties mix, resulting in a new state that conserves mass and energy.

Applications of Psychrometrics

- **HVAC Design and Operation:** Ensuring thermal comfort in residential and commercial buildings through the appropriate control of temperature and humidity.
- **Industrial Processes:** Applications such as pharmaceuticals, food processing, and paper manufacturing, where specific humidity levels are crucial for production quality.
- **Agriculture:** Managing greenhouse environments or storage facilities to optimize conditions for plant growth and food preservation.
- **Meteorology and Climate Science:** Understanding weather patterns and predicting dew formation, fog, or frost.

Challenges in Psychrometrics

1. Accuracy of Measurements: Obtaining precise humidity and temperature readings can be challenging, especially in fluctuating conditions or extreme environments.

2. System Design Complexity: Designing HVAC systems that efficiently handle diverse and dynamic climatic conditions requires sophisticated modeling and control strategies.

3. Energy Efficiency: Balancing humidity control with energy consumption is critical, especially in climates requiring extensive humidification or dehumidification.

Conclusion

Psychrometrics is a vital area of thermodynamics that combines the principles of heat and mass transfer with the chemistry of air-water vapor mixtures. Mastery of psychrometric principles allows engineers to design more effective and efficient HVAC systems, improve industrial processes, and enhance indoor air quality. Understanding these interactions not only helps in creating comfortable living and working environments but also supports sustainability in energy use.

Problems:

Problem 1: Thermodynamic Laws and Equilibrium Calculate the change in internal energy when 500 J of heat is added to a system that does 300 J of work on its surroundings.

Problem 2: Thermodynamic Properties and Processes If a gas expands from 1 m³ to 3 m³ against a constant external pressure of 100 kPa, how much work is done by the gas?

Problem 3: Heat Transfer Methods Determine the heat transfer rate through a 2 m² wall that has a thermal conductivity of 0.5 W/mK, thickness of 0.1 m, with one side at 20°C and the other at 10°C.

Problem 4: Psychrometrics Calculate the dew point temperature when the relative humidity is 50% and the dry bulb temperature is 30°C.

Problem 5: Thermodynamic Laws and Equilibrium A heat engine operates between two reservoirs at 600 K and 300 K. Calculate the maximum possible efficiency of the engine.

Problem 6: Thermodynamic Properties and Processes A cylinder contains 0.03 m³ of nitrogen at 300 K and 500 kPa. Calculate the change in internal energy if the volume is doubled and the pressure remains constant. (Assume nitrogen behaves as an ideal gas and $Cv = 0.741\ kj/kg.KC$)

Problem 7: Heat Transfer Methods How much heat is lost per hour through a glass window 3 m x 2 m, 4 mm thick, if the inside temperature is 22°C and the outside temperature is -3°C? Assume the thermal conductivity of glass is 1 W/mK.

Problem 8: Psychrometrics If the specific humidity of the air is 0.0075 kg of water per kg of dry air and the total pressure is 101 kPa, calculate the partial pressure of the water vapor.

Problem 9: Thermodynamic Properties and Processes Estimate the speed of sound in air at $300\ K\ using\ \gamma = 1.4\ and\ R = 287 J/kg.K$.

Problem 10: Heat Transfer Methods Calculate the convective heat transfer coefficient if 500 W of power is required to maintain a heated plate at 120°C in a room where the air is at 25°C and the surface area of the plate is 0.5 m².

Solutions:

Solution 1:
$$\Delta U = Q - W = 500\,J - 300\,J = 200\,J$$

Solution 2:
$$W = P\Delta V = 100\,\text{kPa} \times (3\,m^3 - 1\,m^3) = 200\,\text{kJ}$$

Solution 3:
$$Q = \frac{kA(T_1-T_2)}{L} = \frac{0.5 \times 2 \times (20-10)}{0.1} = 100 \text{ W}$$

Solution 4:
This requires using a psychrometric chart or formula based on the saturation pressure at 30°C. Assume saturation pressure is 4.24 kPa:
$$T_{dp} = T - \left(\frac{100-RH}{5}\right) \approx 30 - (100-50)/5 = 20 \,^\circ\text{C}$$

Solution 5:
$$\eta = 1 - \frac{T_{cold}}{T_{hot}} = 1 - \frac{300}{600} = 0.5 \text{ or } 50\%$$

Solution 6:
Assuming ideal gas behavior, the change in internal energy for an isobaric process is zero for an ideal gas.

Solution 7:
$$Q = \frac{kA(T_1-T_2)}{L} = \frac{1 \times 6 \times (22-(-3))}{0.004} \times 3600 = 47,250 \text{ kWh}$$

Solution 8:
Using Dalton's Law of partial pressures:
$$P_{water} = \text{Total pressure} \times \text{Specific humidity} = 101 \times 0.0075 = 0.7575 \text{ kPa}$$

Solution 9:
$$c = \sqrt{\gamma RT} = \sqrt{1.4 \times 287 \times 300} \approx 347 \text{ m/s}$$

Solution 10:
$$h = \frac{Q}{A\Delta T} = \frac{500}{0.5 \times (120-25)} = 8.33 \text{ W/m}^2\text{K}$$

FREE SUPPLEMENTARY RESOURCES

Scan the QR code below to download the eBooks:

☑ Full Length Practice Test
☑ 13 E-Learning Videos
☑ 250+ Problems with Detailed Solutions

SCAN THE QR CODE TO DOWNLOAD

COMPLEMENTARY RESOURCES

Why Your Support Matters for This Book:

Creating this book has been an unexpectedly tough journey, more so than even the most complex coding sessions. For the first time, I've faced the daunting challenge of writer's block. While I understand the subject matter, translating it into clear, logical, and engaging writing is another matter altogether.

Moreover, my choice to bypass traditional publishers has led me to embrace the role of an 'independent author.' This path has had its hurdles, yet my commitment to helping others remains strong.

This is why your feedback on Amazon would be incredibly valuable. Your thoughts and opinions not only matter greatly to me, but they also play a crucial role in spreading the word about this book. Here's what I suggest:

1. **If you haven't done so already, scan the QR code at the beginning of the book to download the** FREE SUPPLEMENTARY RESOURCES.

2. **Scan the QR code below and quickly leave feedback on Amazon!**

The optimal approach? Consider making a brief video to share your impressions of the book! If that's a bit much, don't worry at all. Just leaving a feedback and including a few photos of the book would be fantastic too!

Note: There's no obligation whatsoever, but it would be immensely valued!

I'm thrilled to embark on this journey with you. Are you prepared to delve in?
Enjoy your reading!

Conclusion

As the final page turns in this comprehensive guide to mastering the FE Other Disciplines Exam, envision yourself stepping confidently into the examination room, equipped with the profound knowledge and understanding that each chapter has bestowed upon you. From the meticulous intricacies of mathematics—spanning analytic geometry to single-variable calculus—to the dynamic principles of fluid mechanics and the robust theories underpinning thermodynamics, your journey through this book has sculpted you into a formidable contender for the exam.

Imagine the diverse array of questions you will encounter, each one a stepping stone towards your professional license. You've delved deep into the core of engineering ethics, navigated through the complexities of electrical circuits, and embraced the critical importance of safety, health, and environmental standards. You've explored the economic strategies that drive project selection and risk management, all while mastering the static and dynamic challenges that mechanical forces present.

With each chapter, your skills have been honed: you can now calculate the stresses in a beam with the same ease as predicting the economic feasibility of an engineering project. The diagrams of forces and systems that once seemed daunting are now clear maps you can navigate effortlessly. Your understanding of material properties has been transformed, enabling you to select the optimal substance for any application with precision and confidence.

As you close this book, picture the exam ahead not as a hurdle, but as a celebration of your dedication and hard work—a test where each question offers a chance to demonstrate the depth and breadth of your engineering prowess. Envision walking out of the exam room, not just as a test taker, but as a professional stepping firmly towards a future where the challenges of the world are met with your newly sharpened skills, ready to innovate, improve, and lead in the field of engineering. This is not just an end but a beginning—the start of a promising career built on the solid foundation of knowledge and understanding you have gained.

Made in the USA
Coppell, TX
22 May 2025